Jumbo
Coloring Pad
Animals

Coloring Pages for Kids

**All rights reserved. No part of this document may be reproduced
Used or transmitted in any form or by any means, electronic or otherwise. This means you
cannot photocopy any material ideas or tips that are provided in this book.**

Coloring Pages for Kids
An imprint of Ciparum LLC

Jumbo Coloring Pad Animals
© 2017 Ciparum LLC
ISBN-10:1-63589-343-7
ISBN-13:978-1-63589-343-4

Coloring Pages for Kids

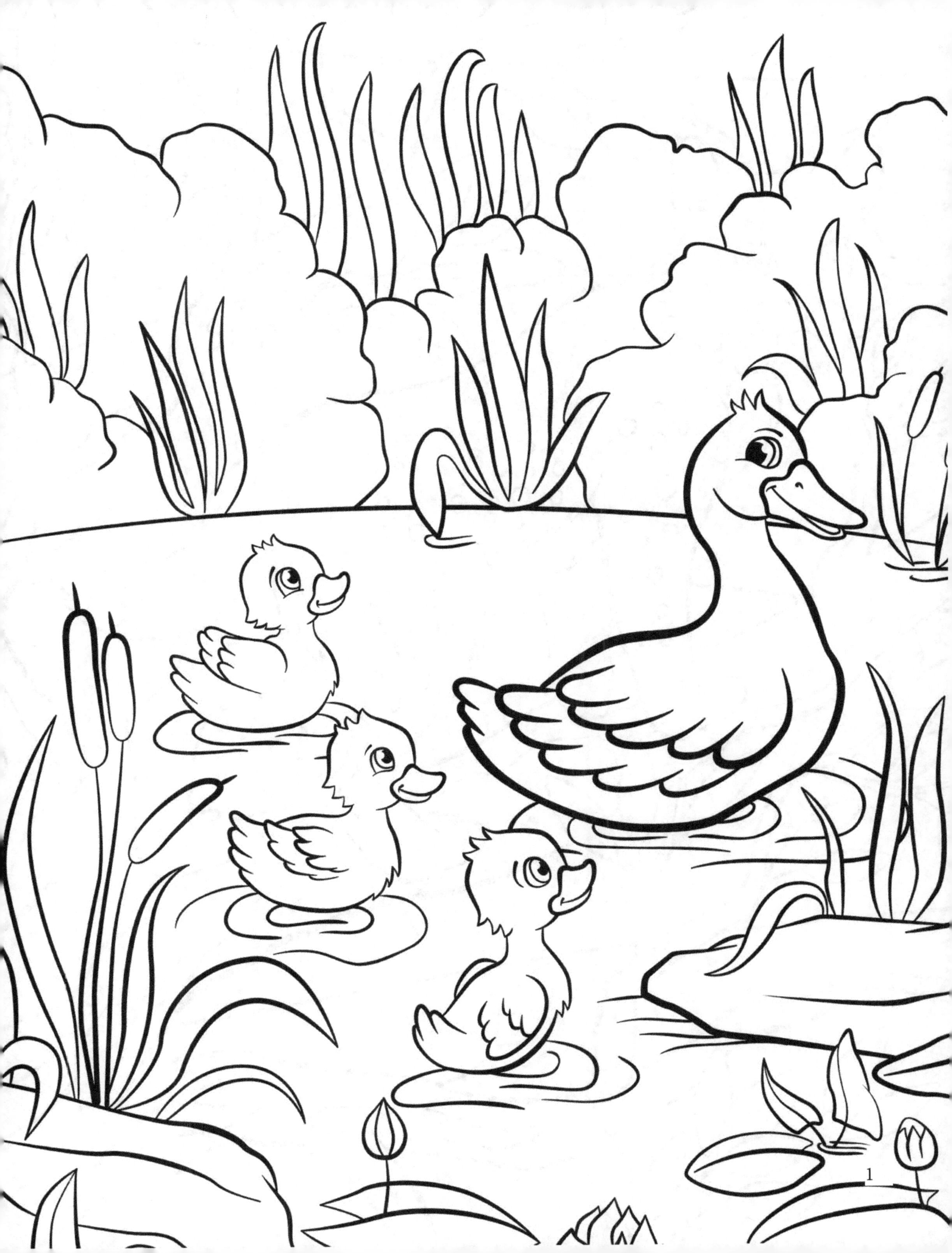

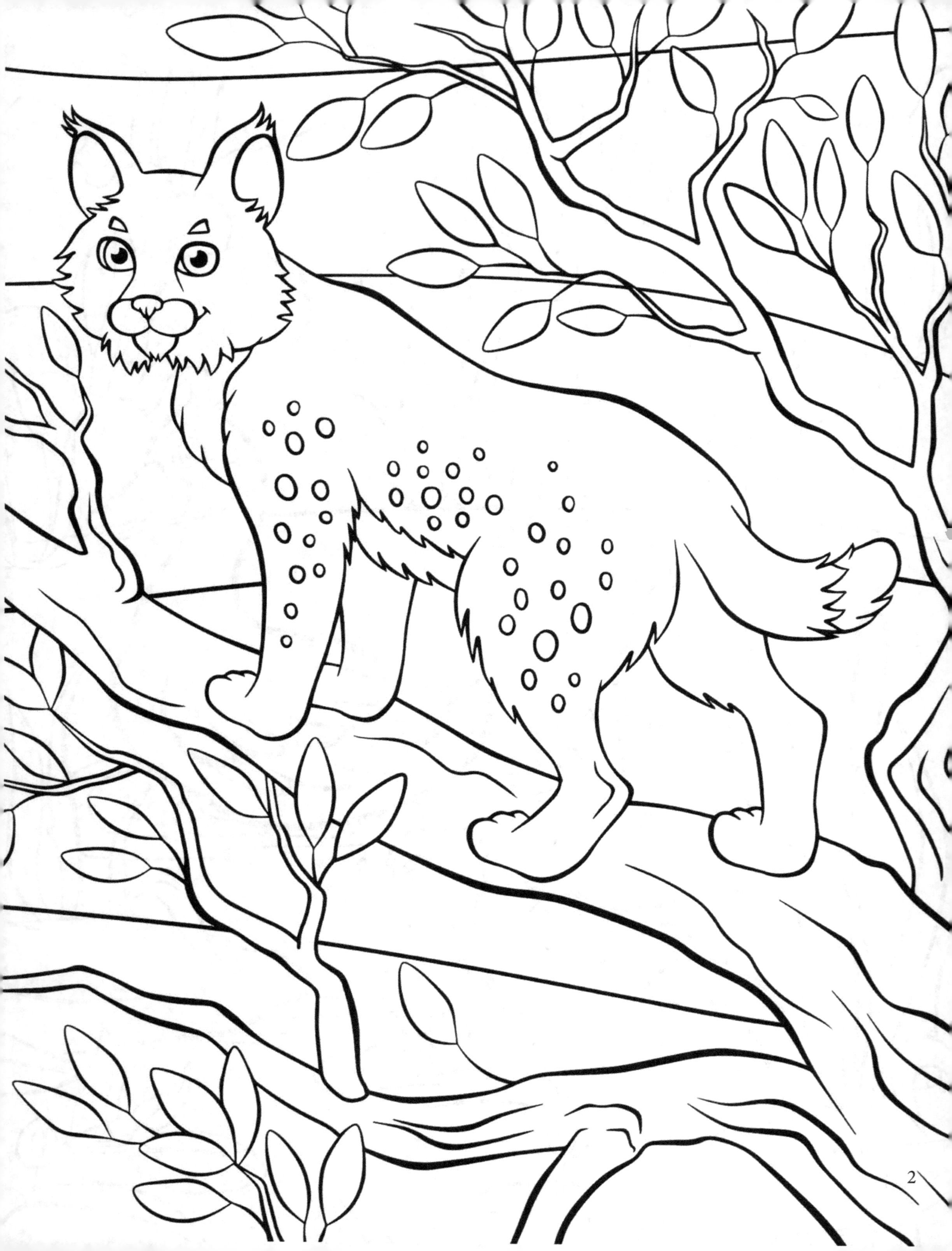

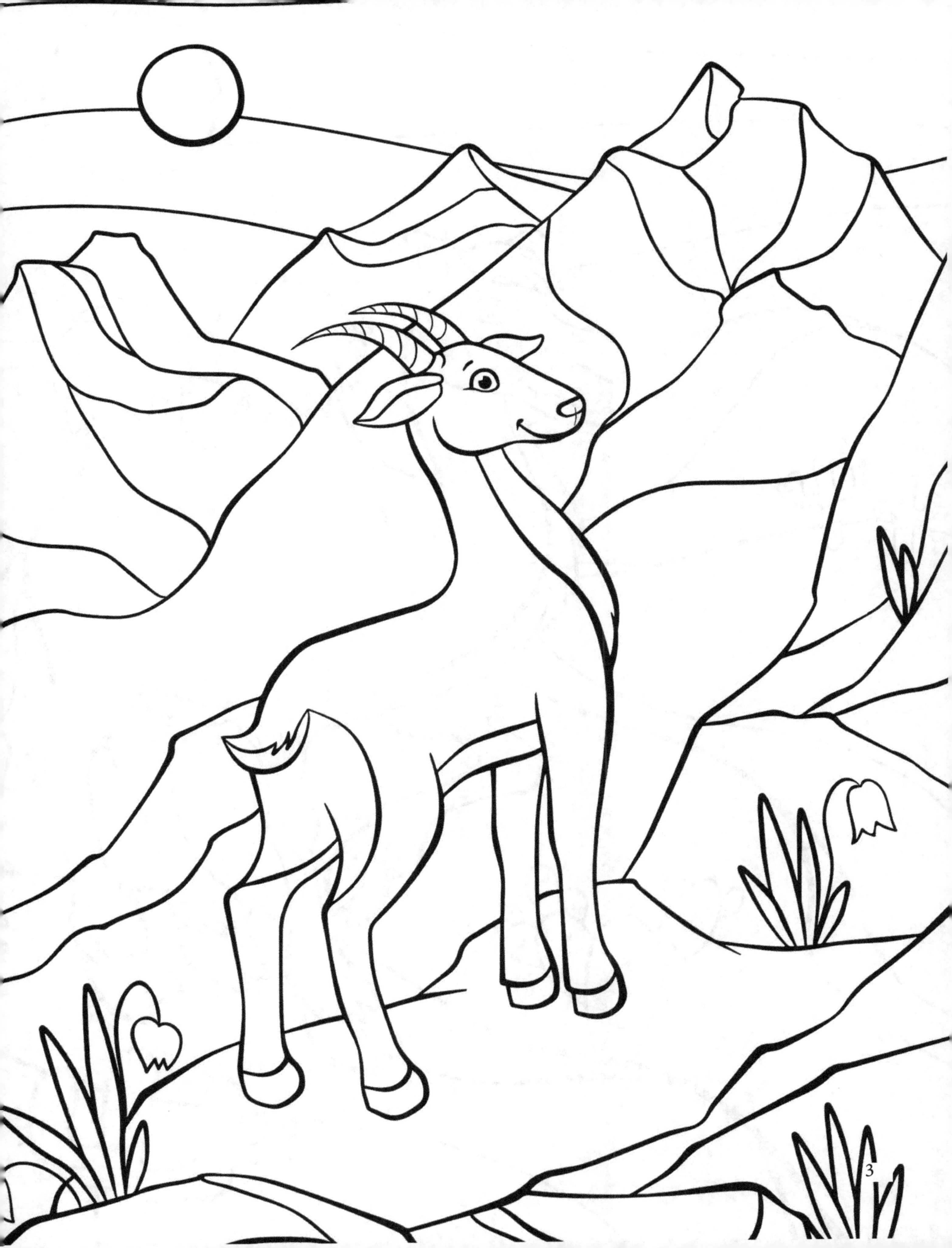

3

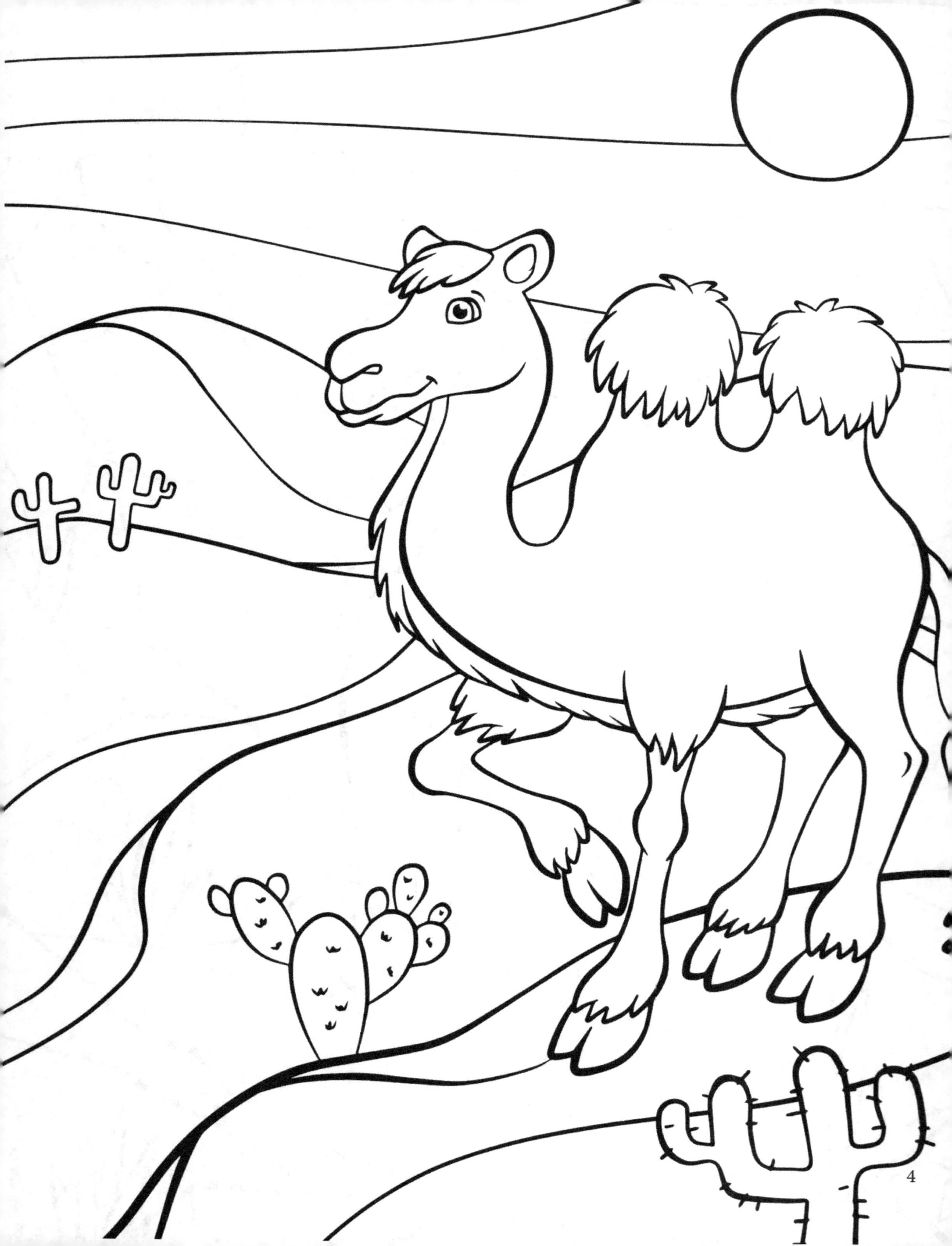

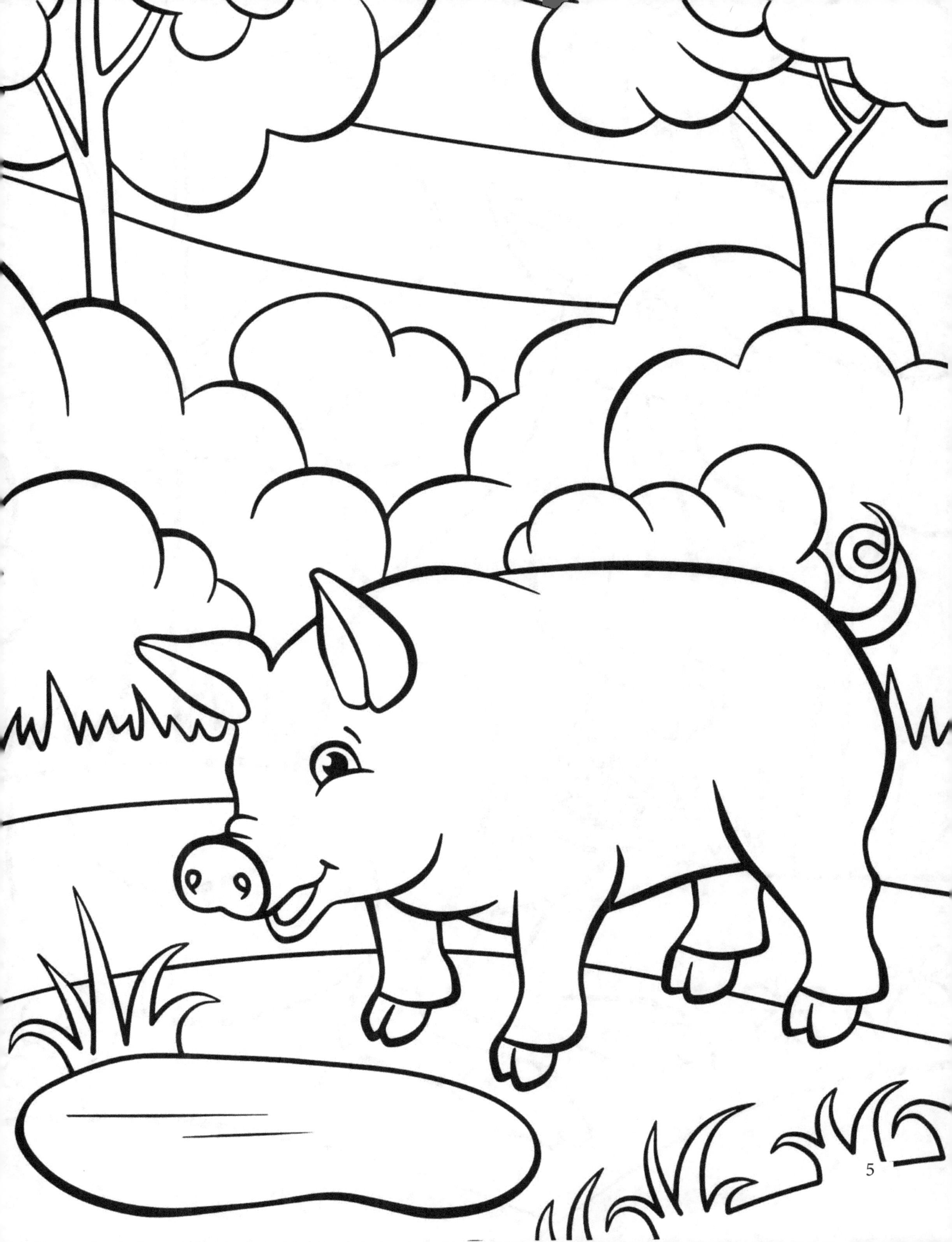

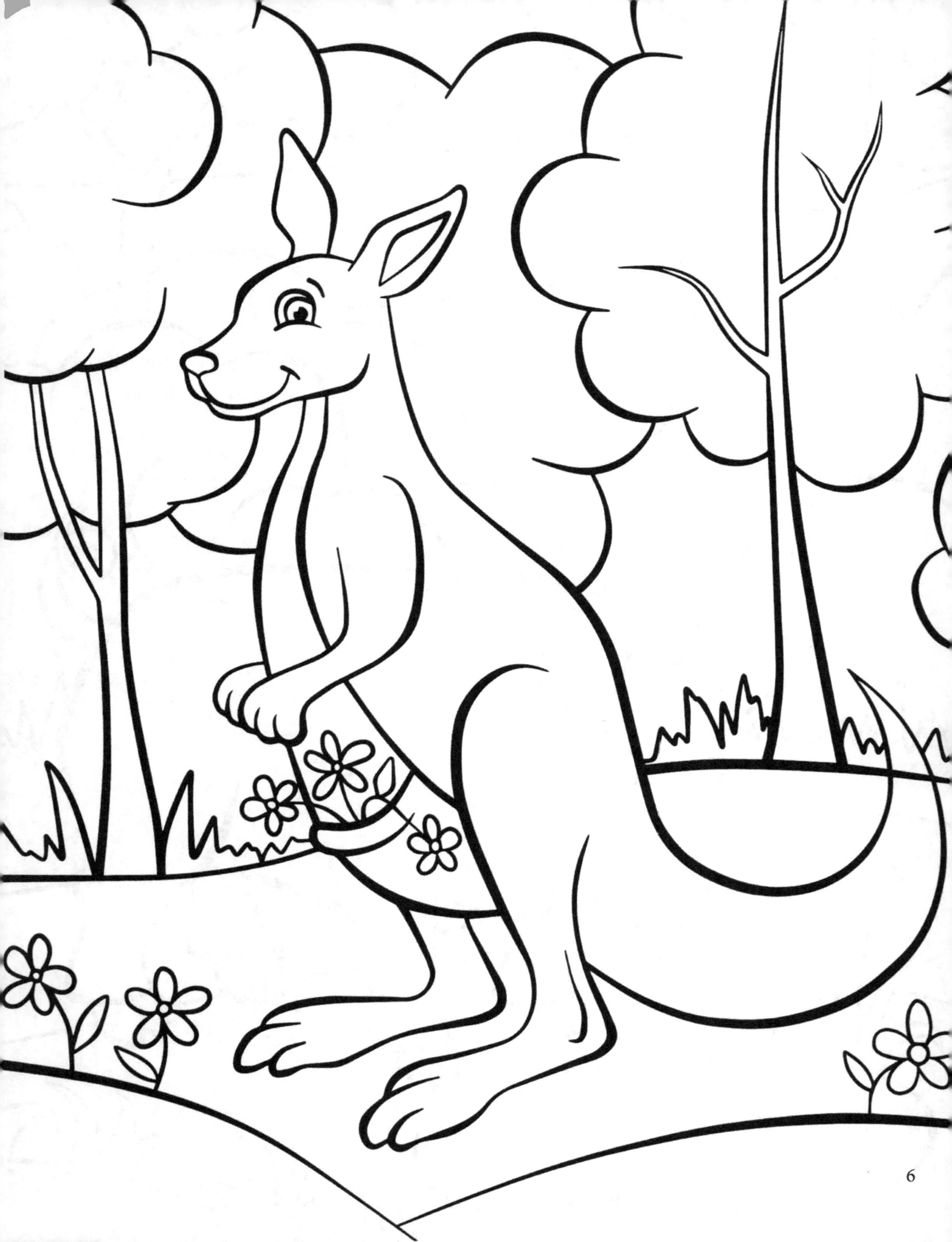

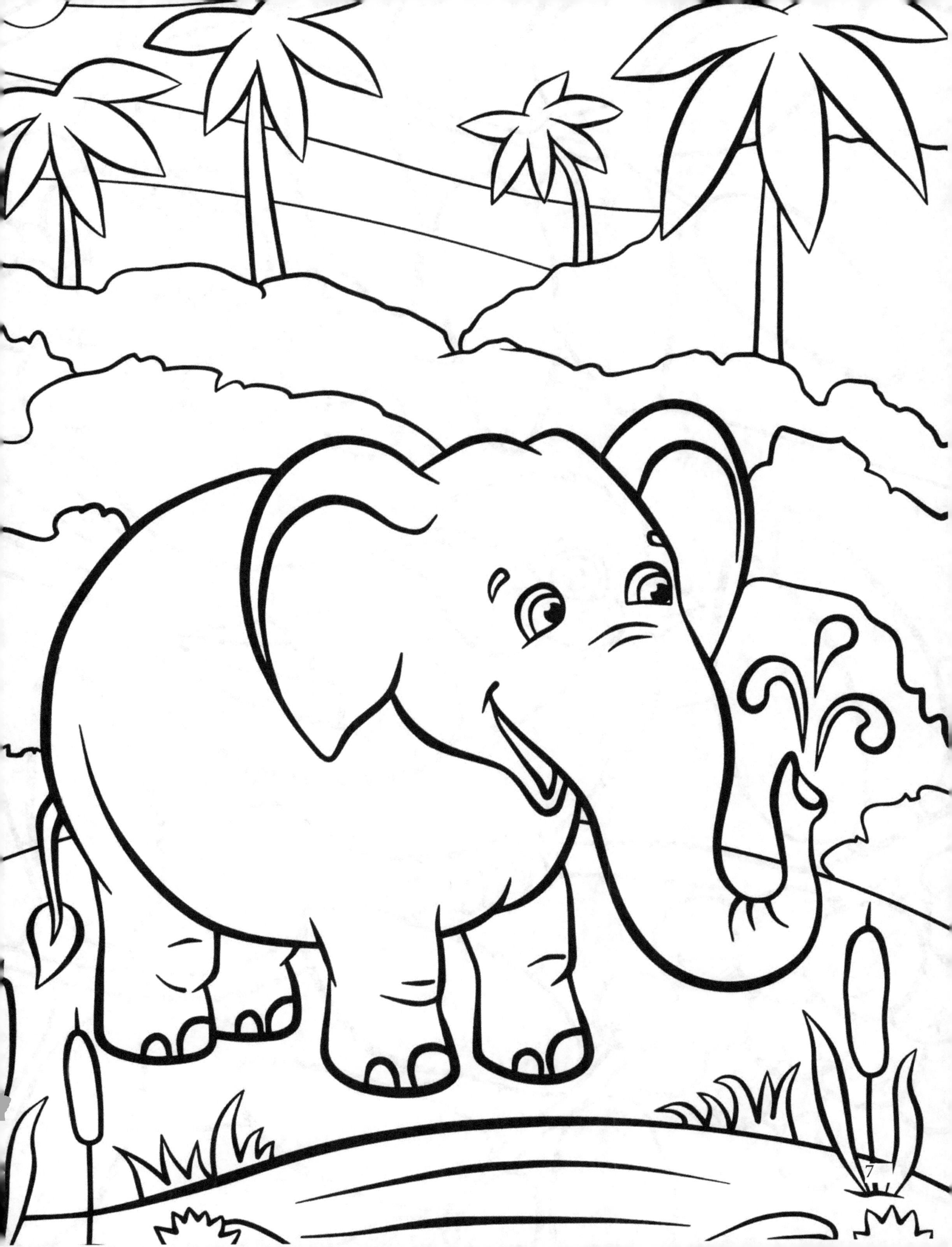
7

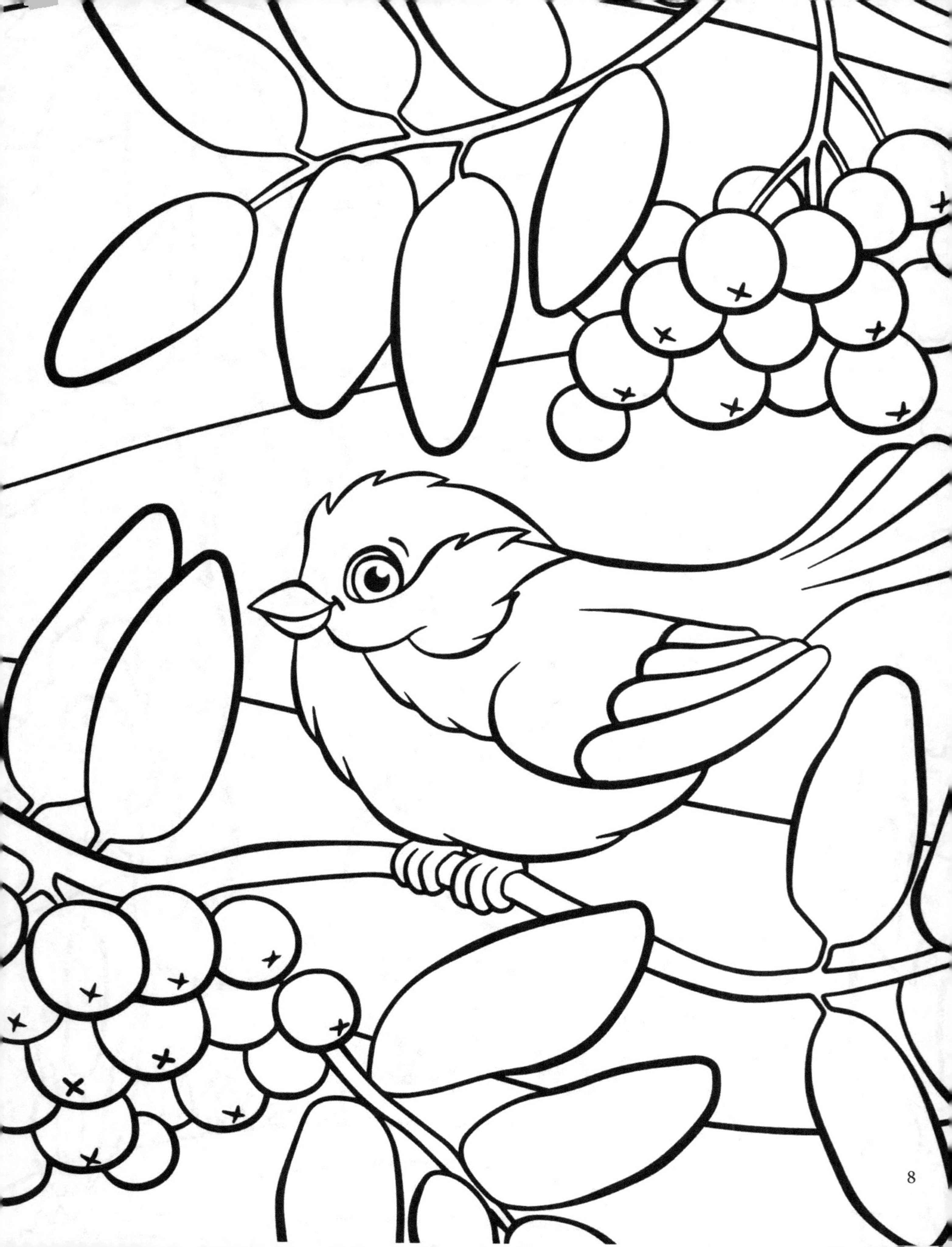

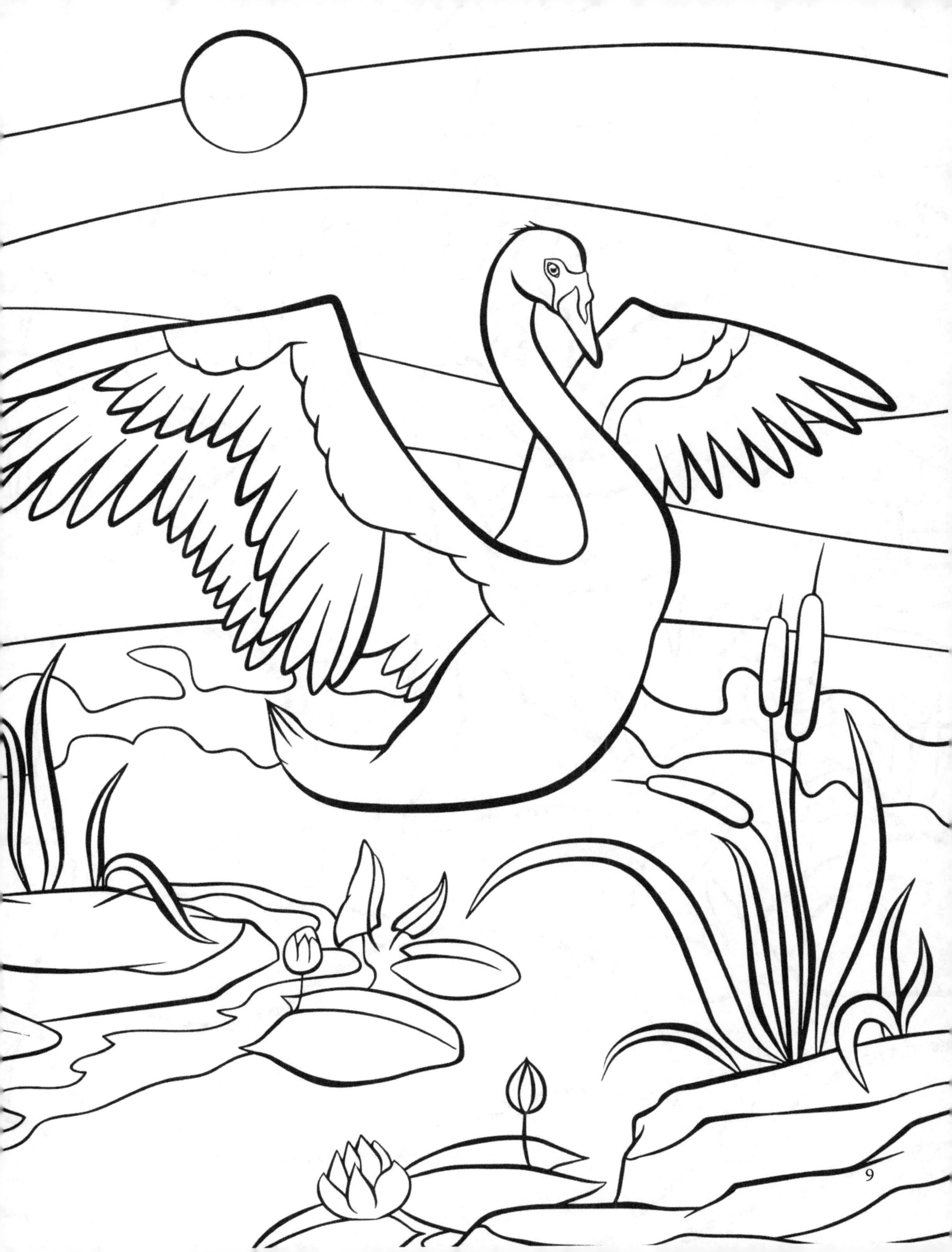

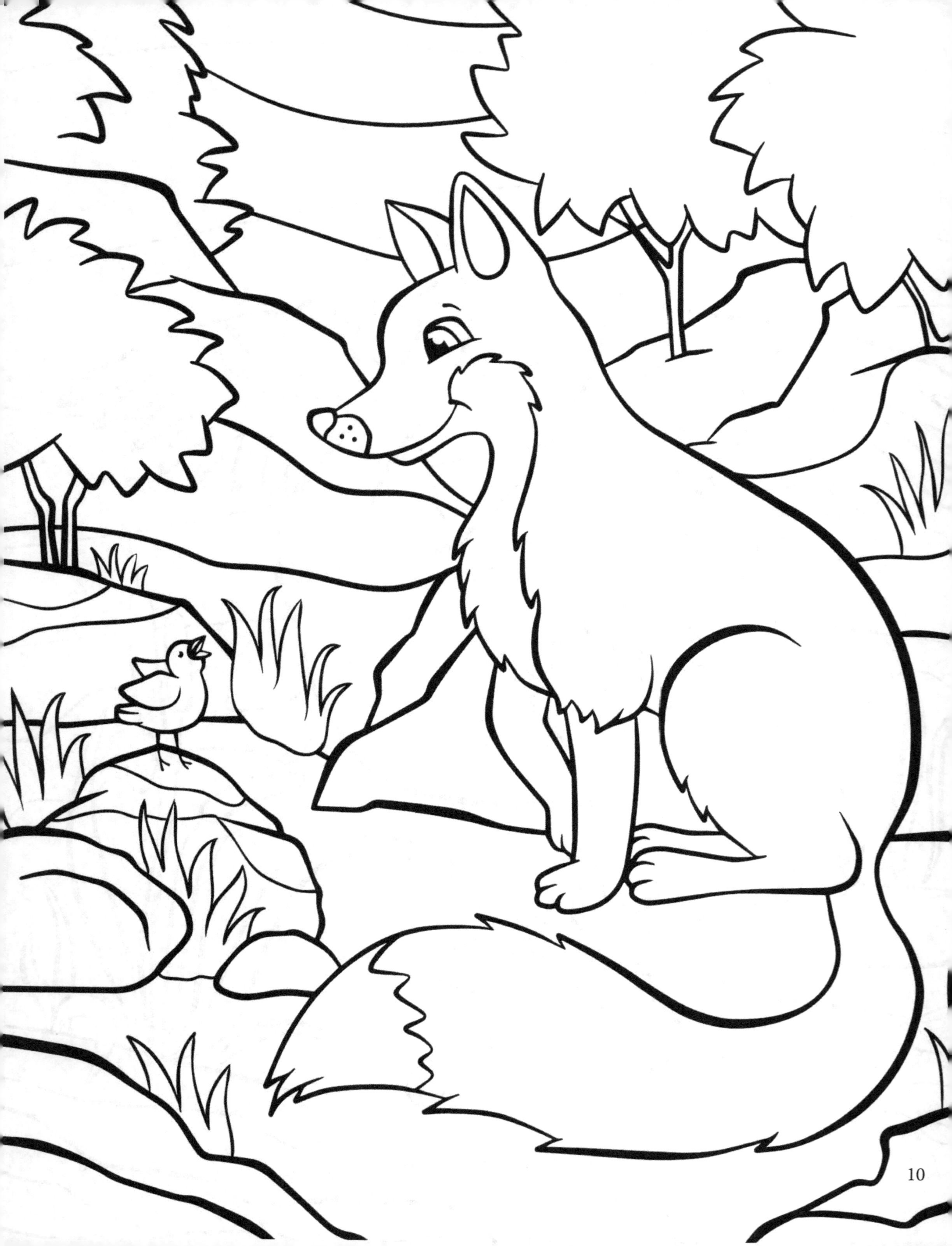

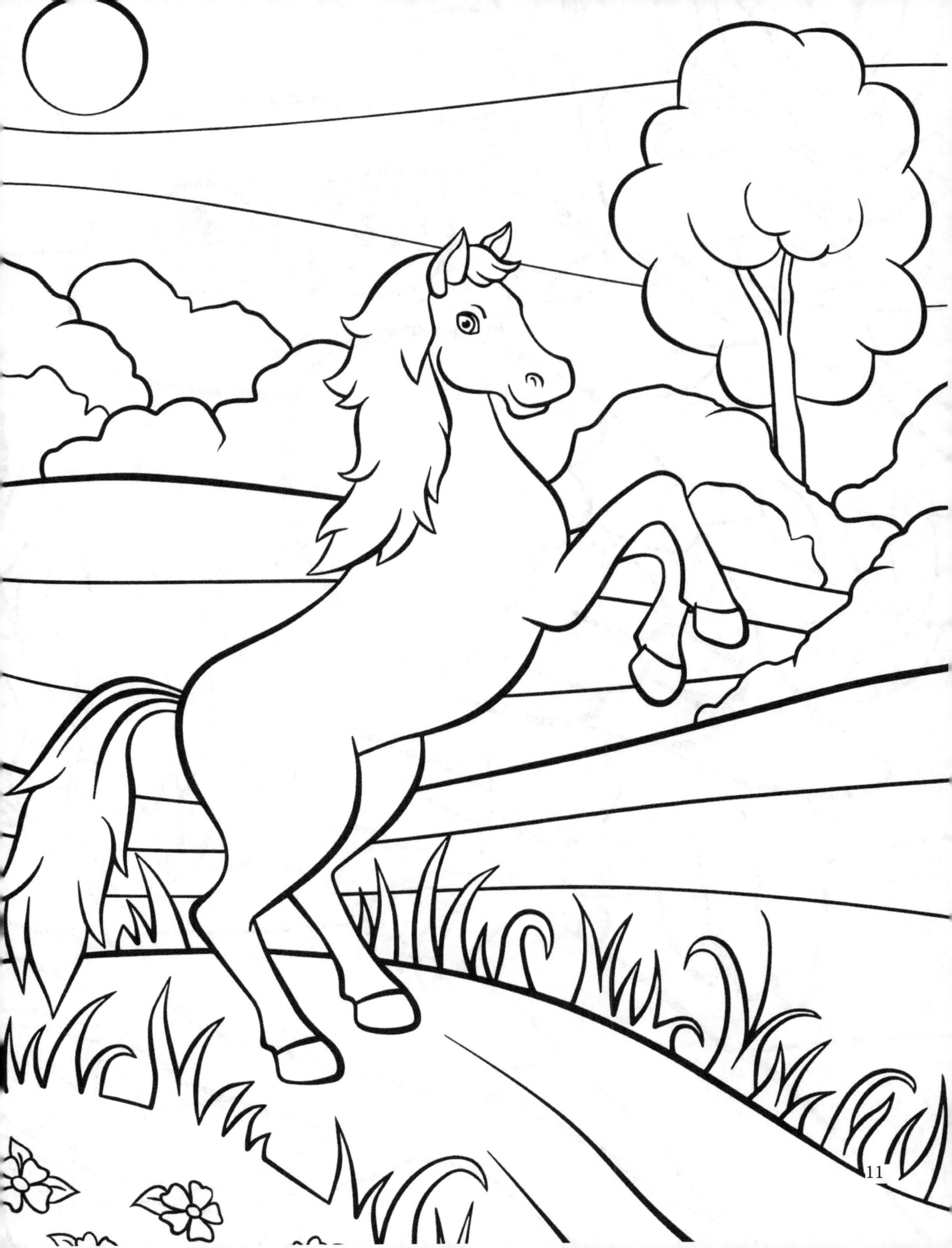

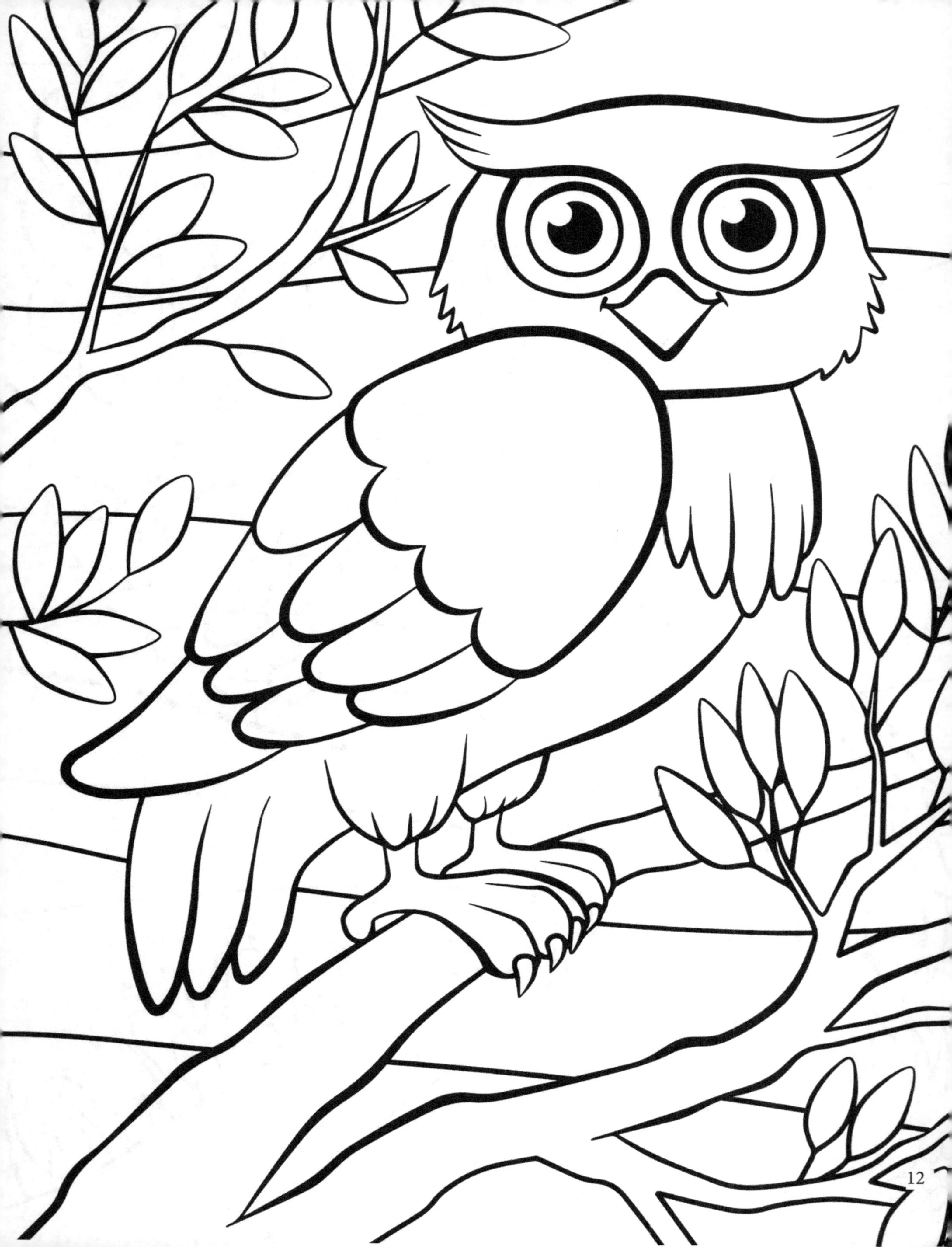

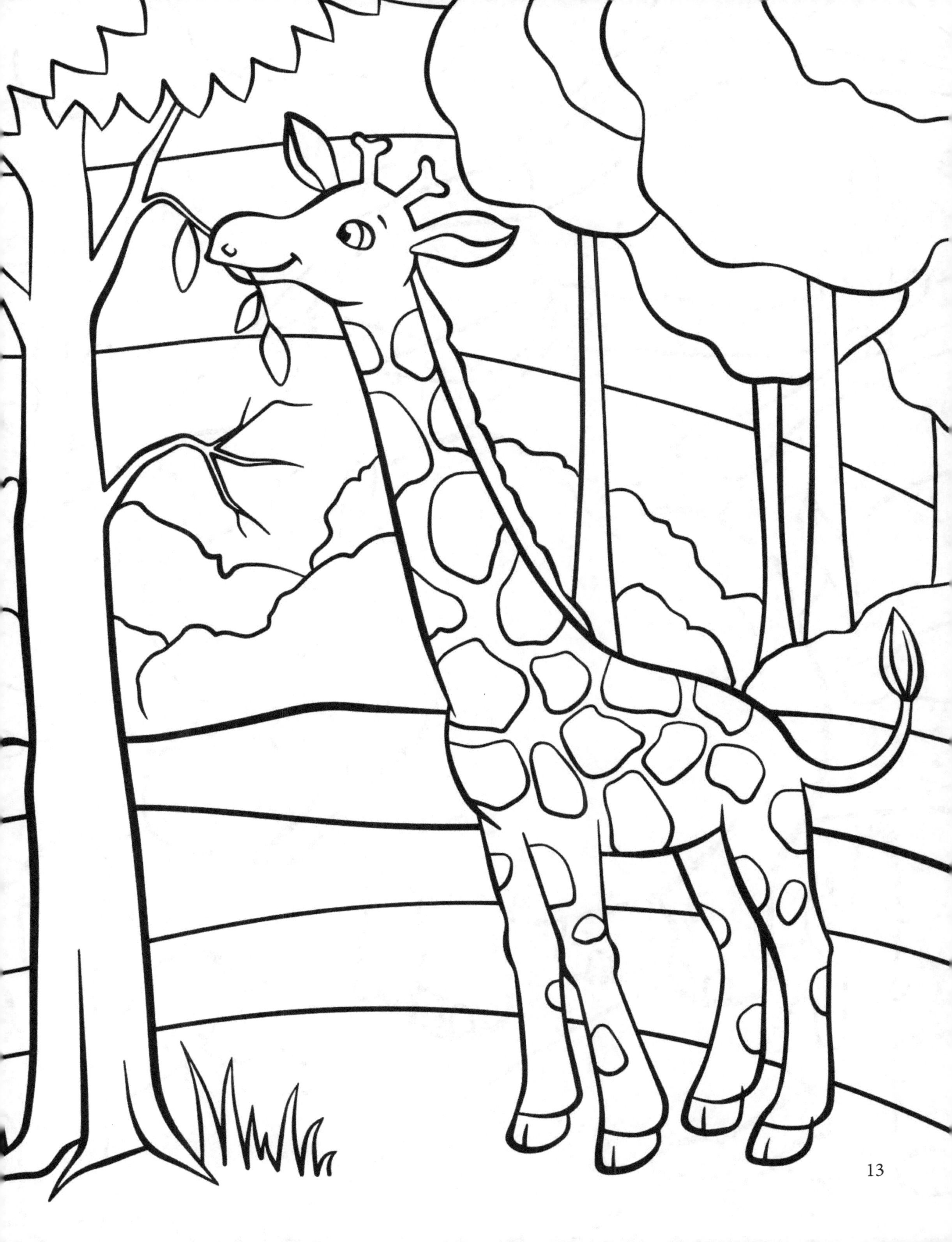

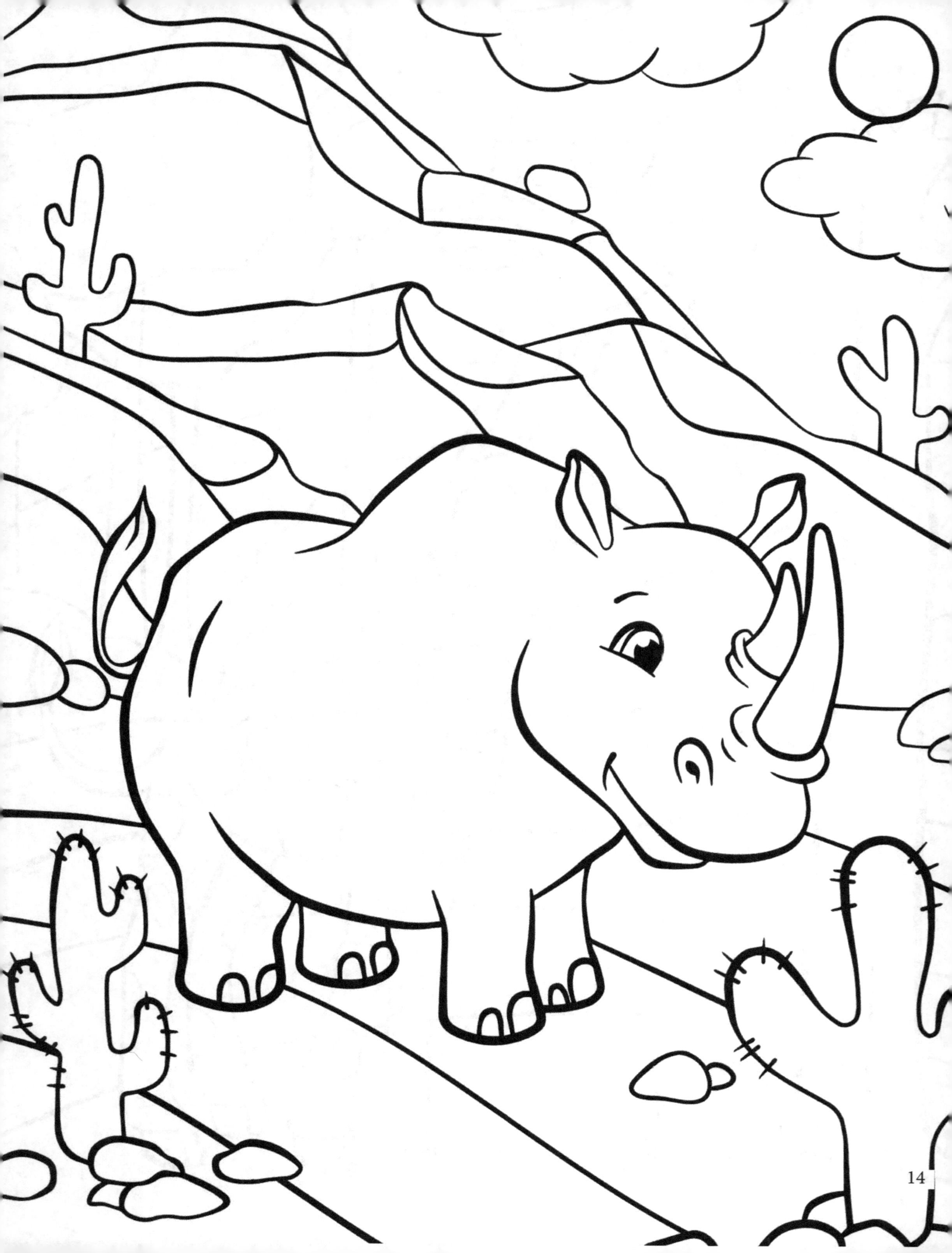

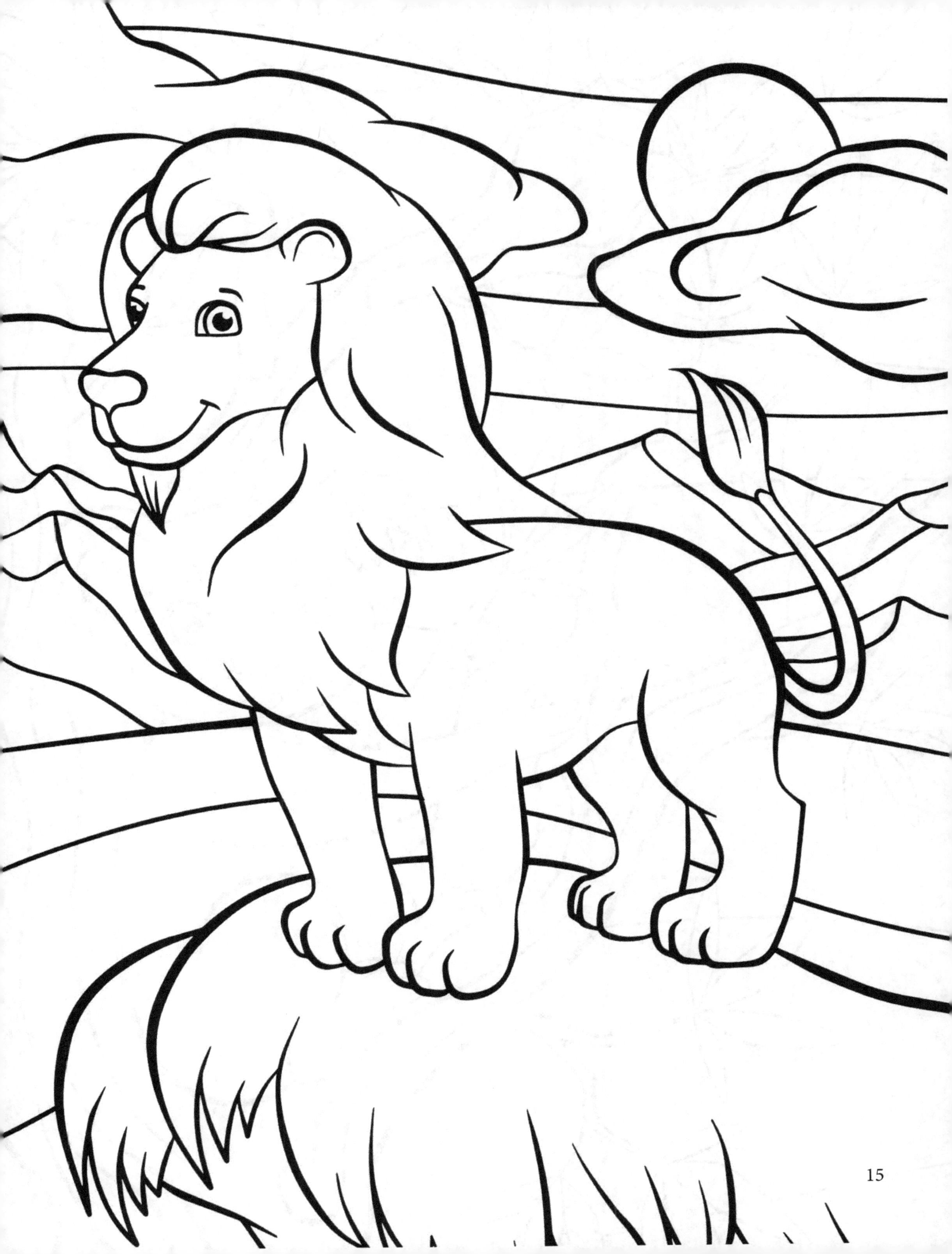

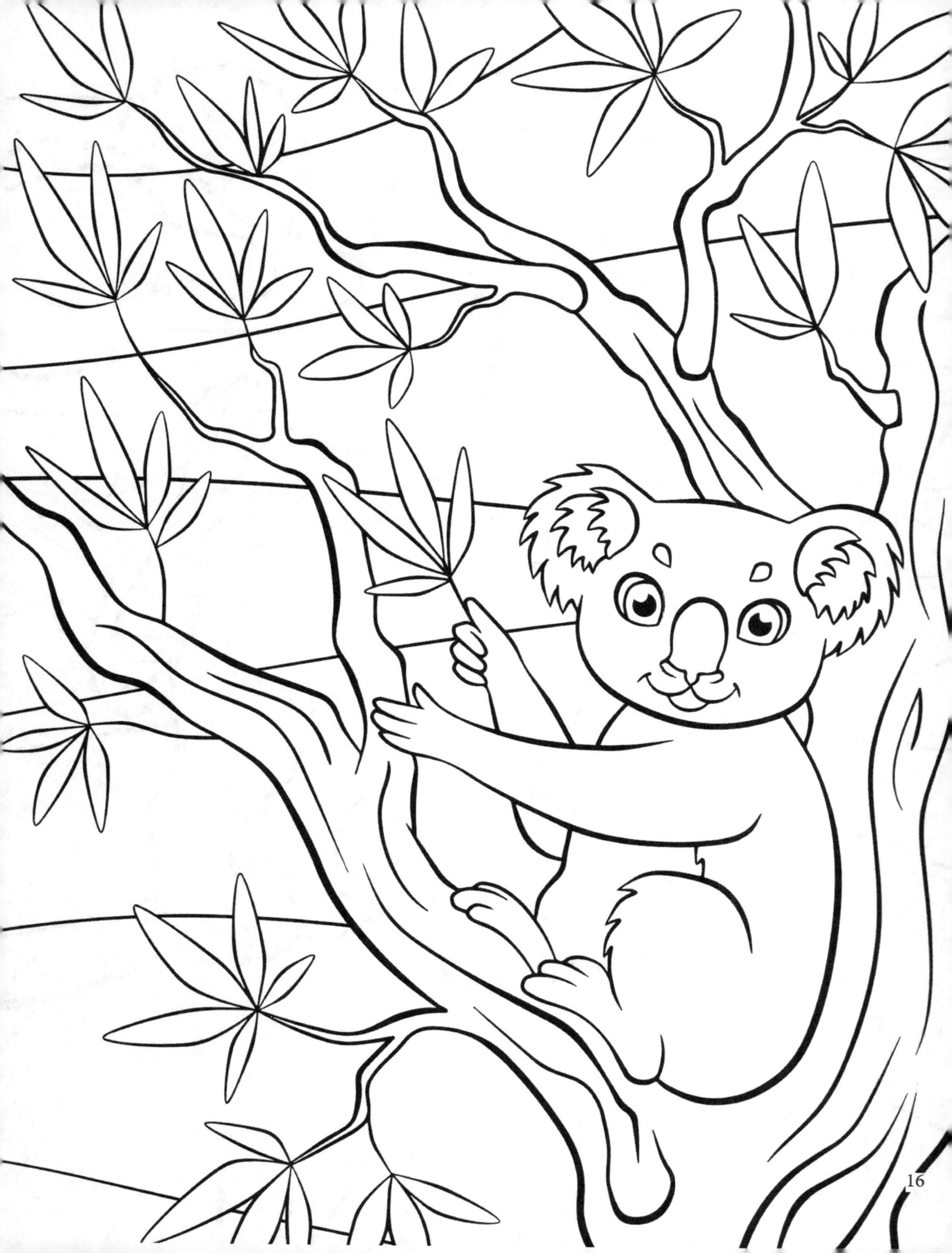

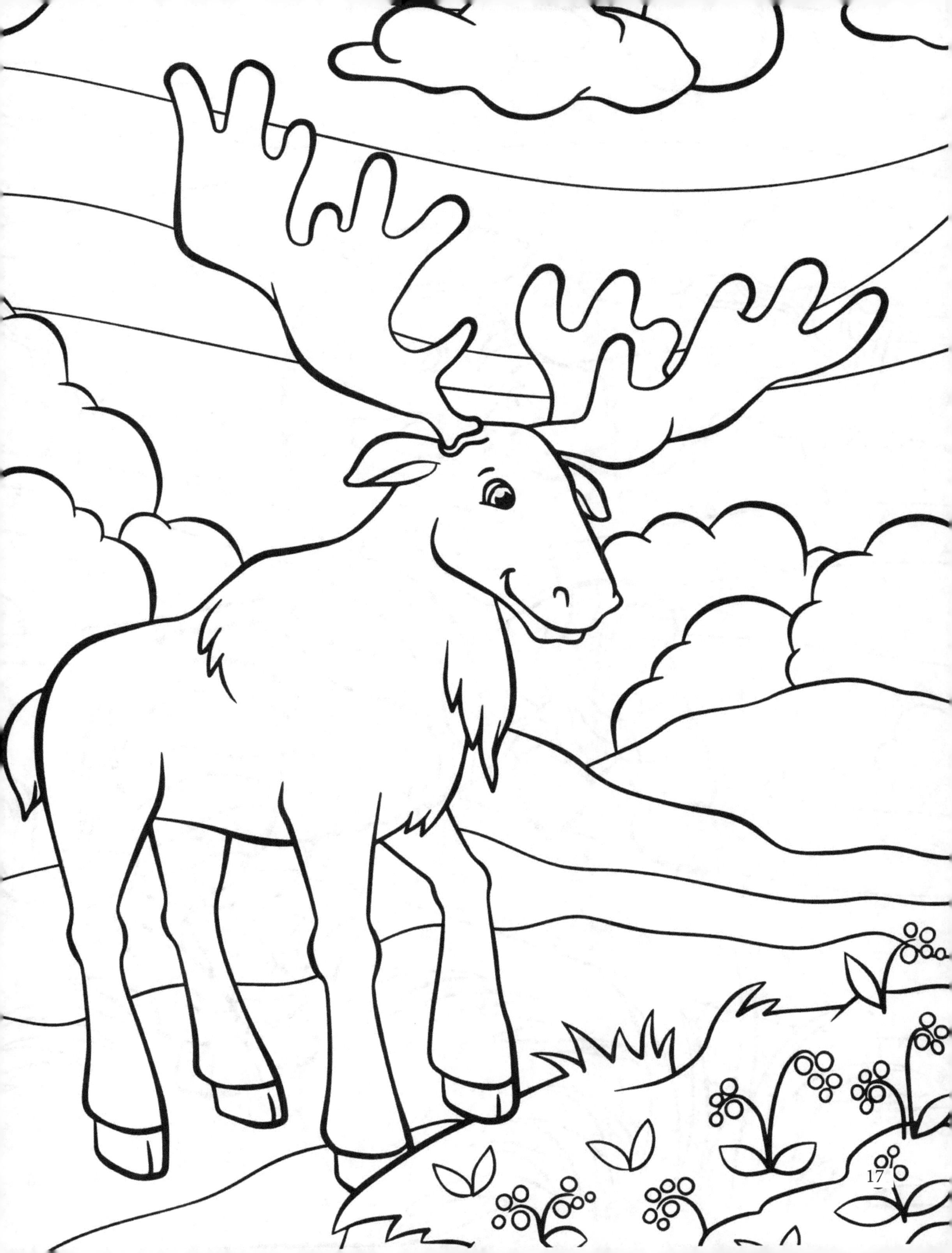

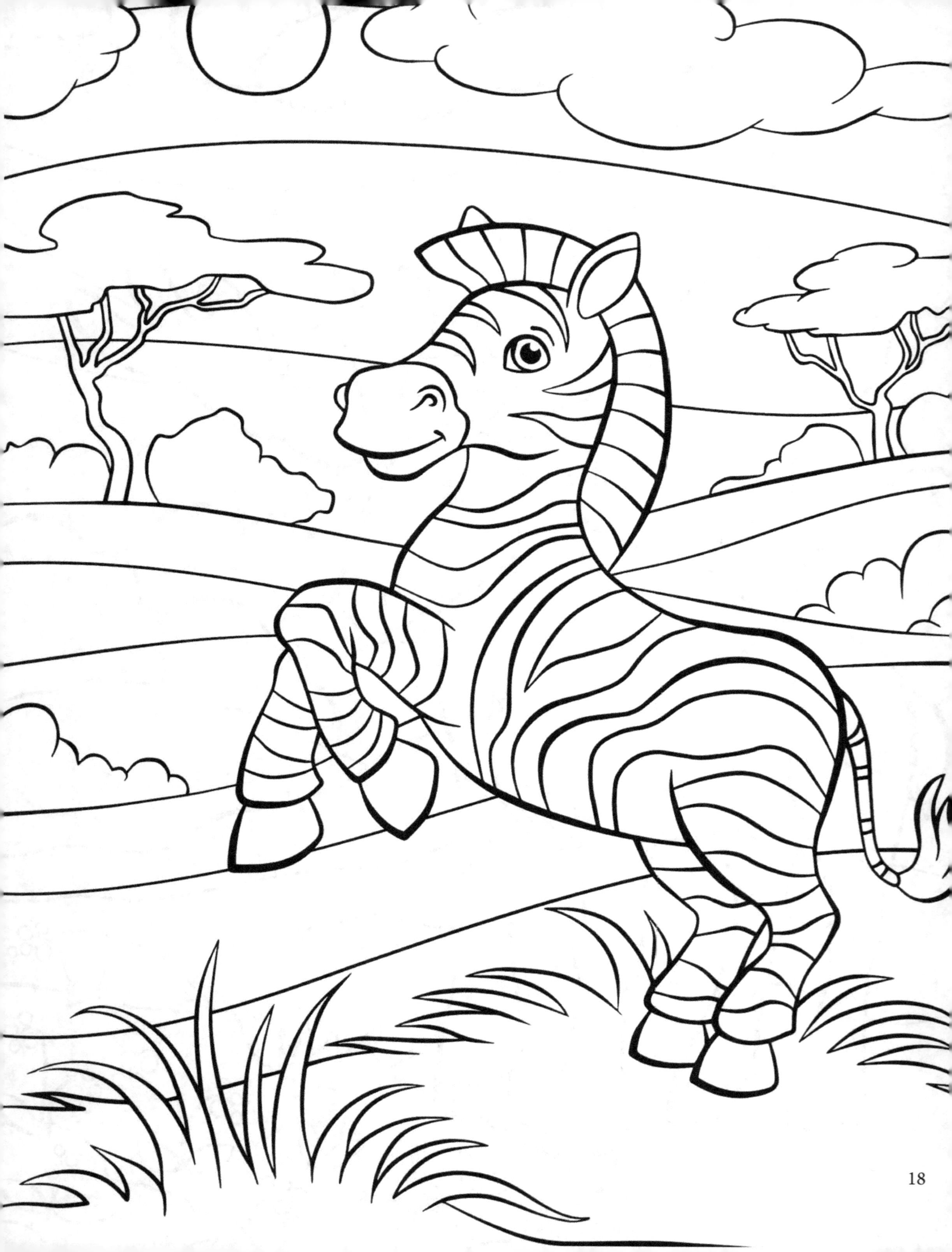

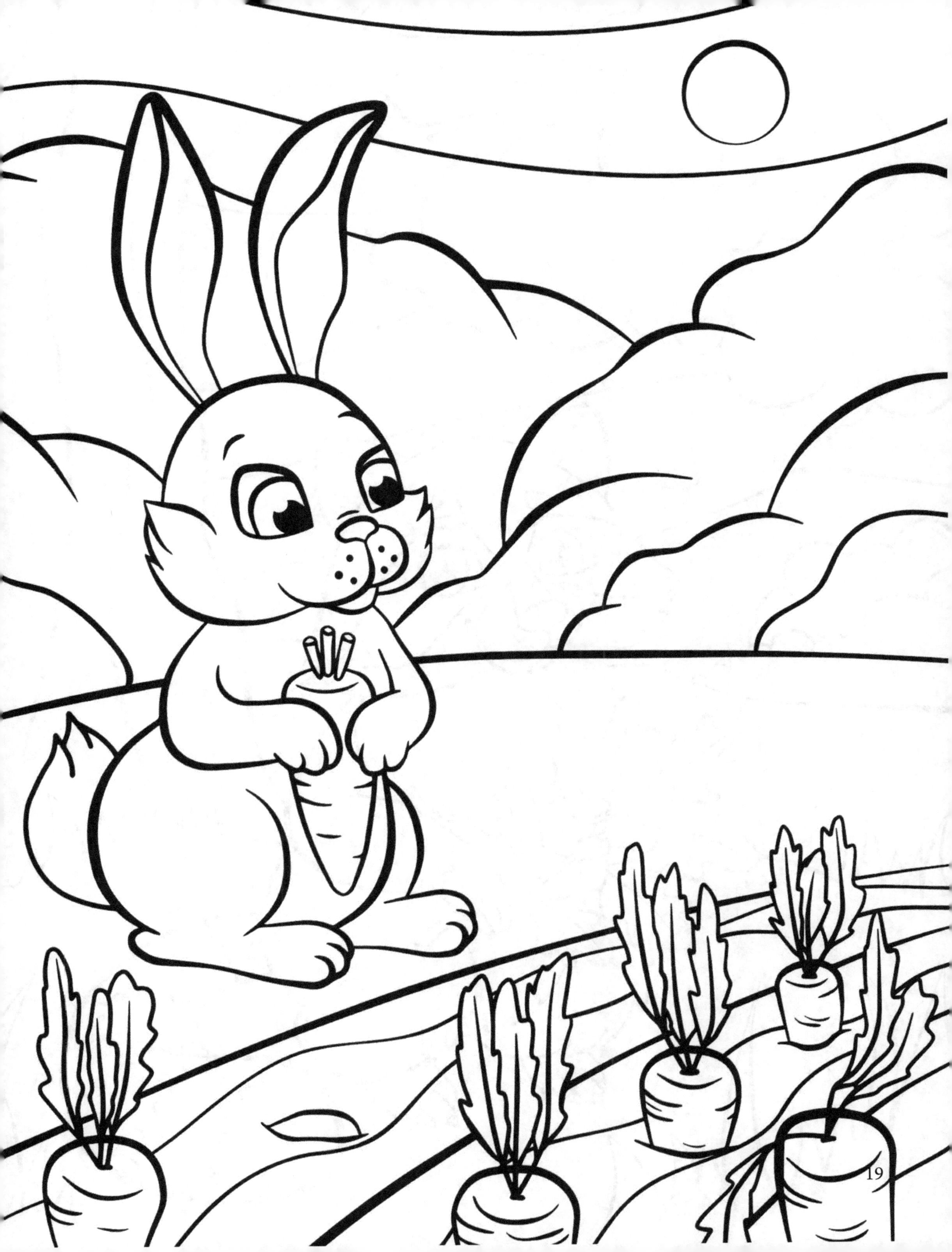

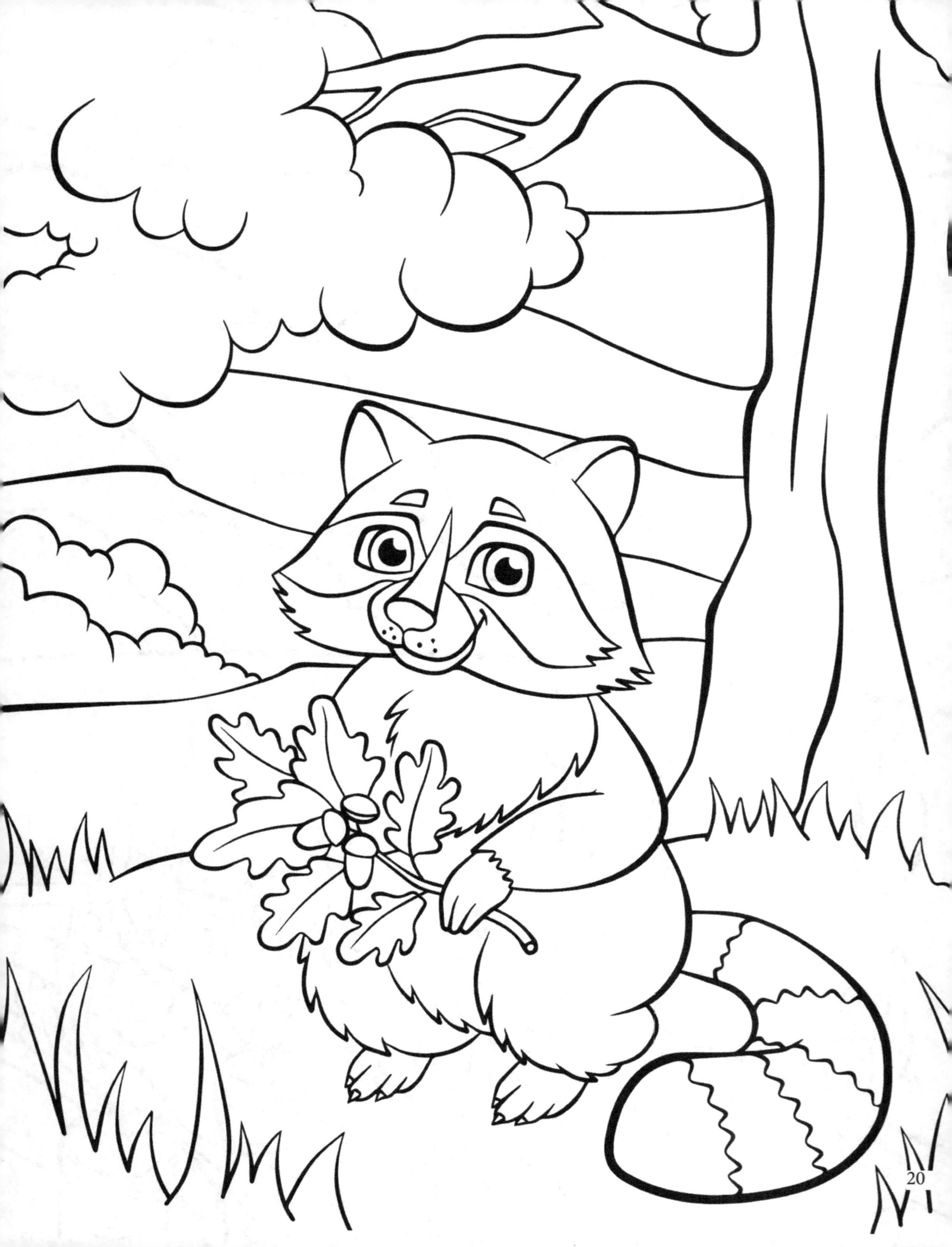

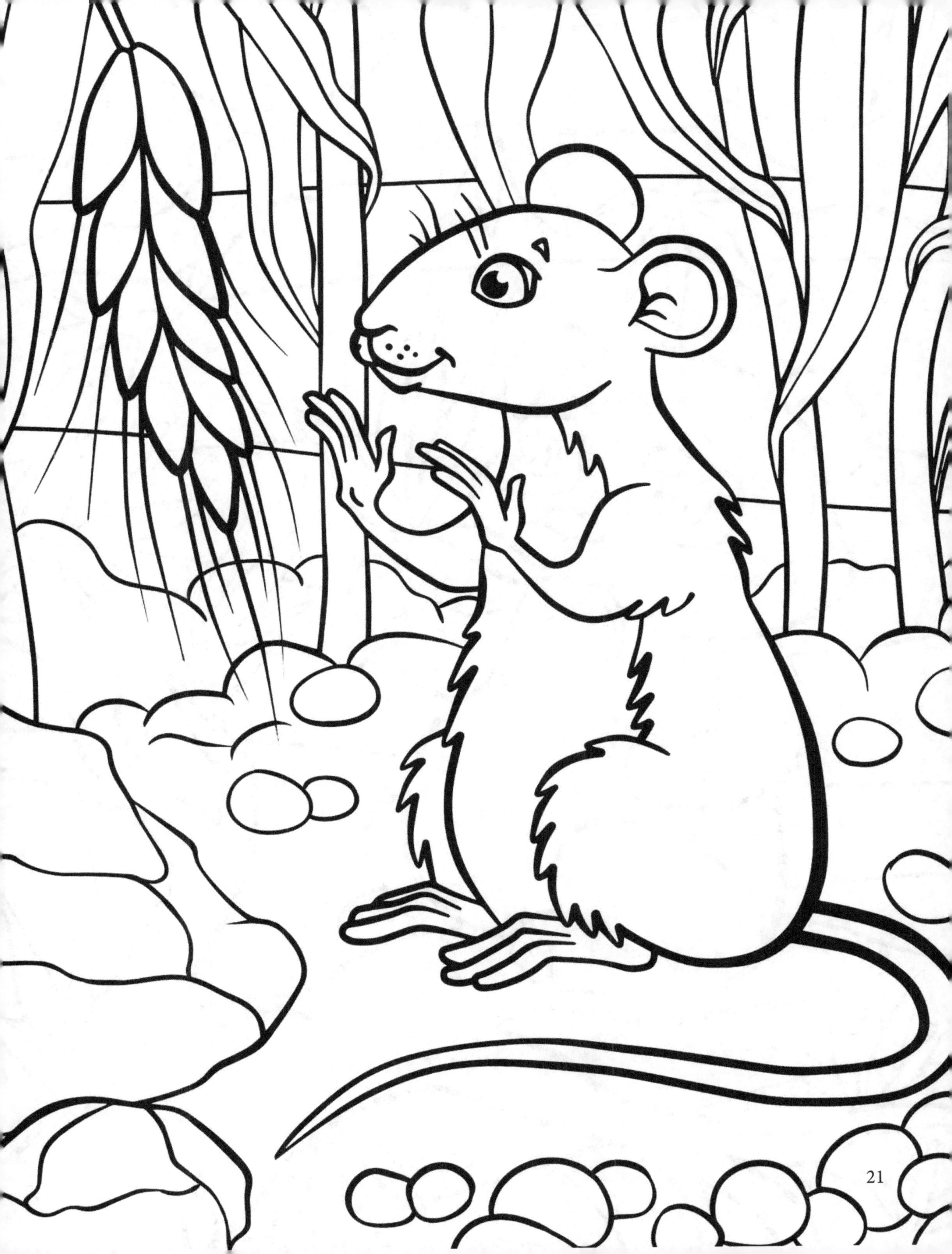

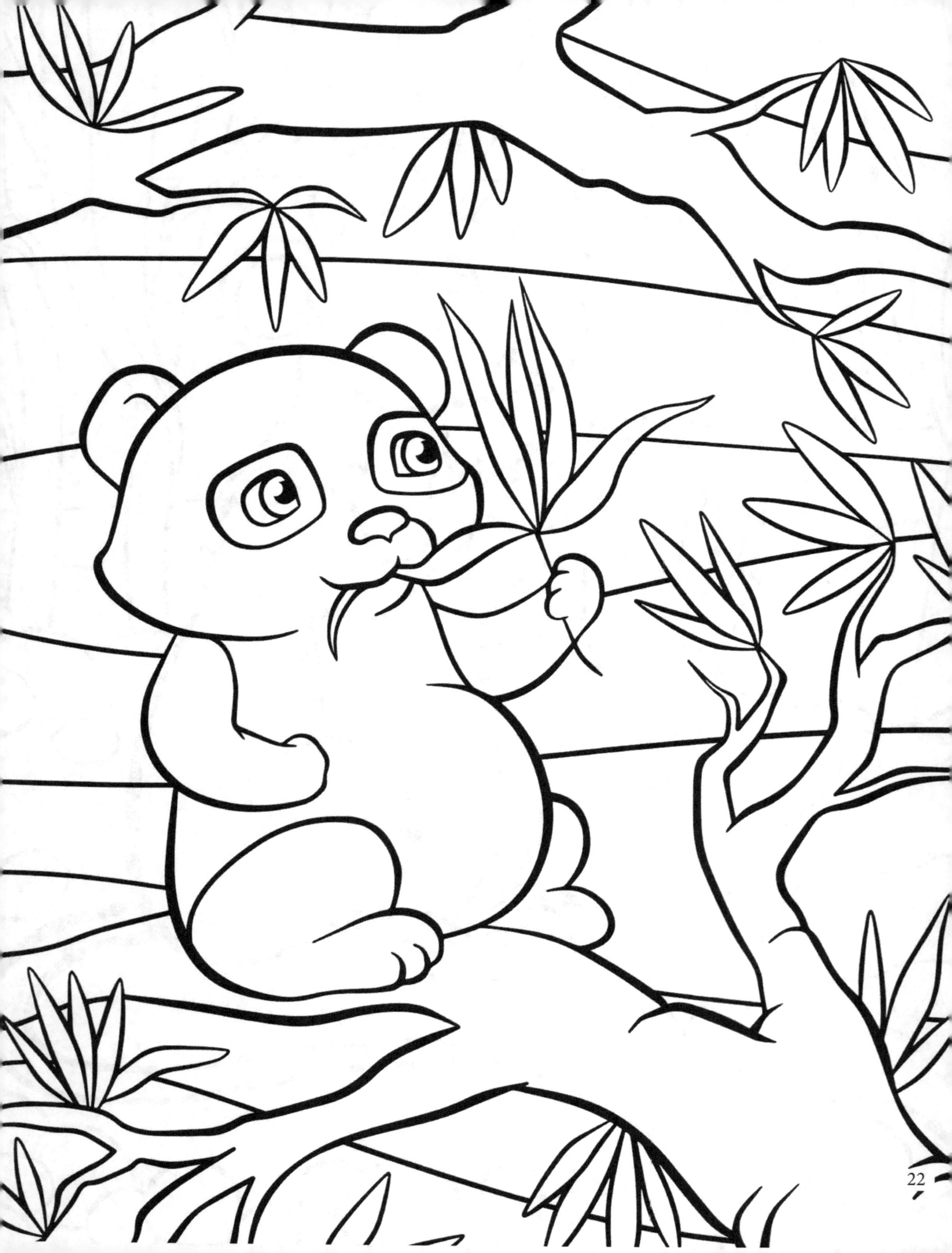

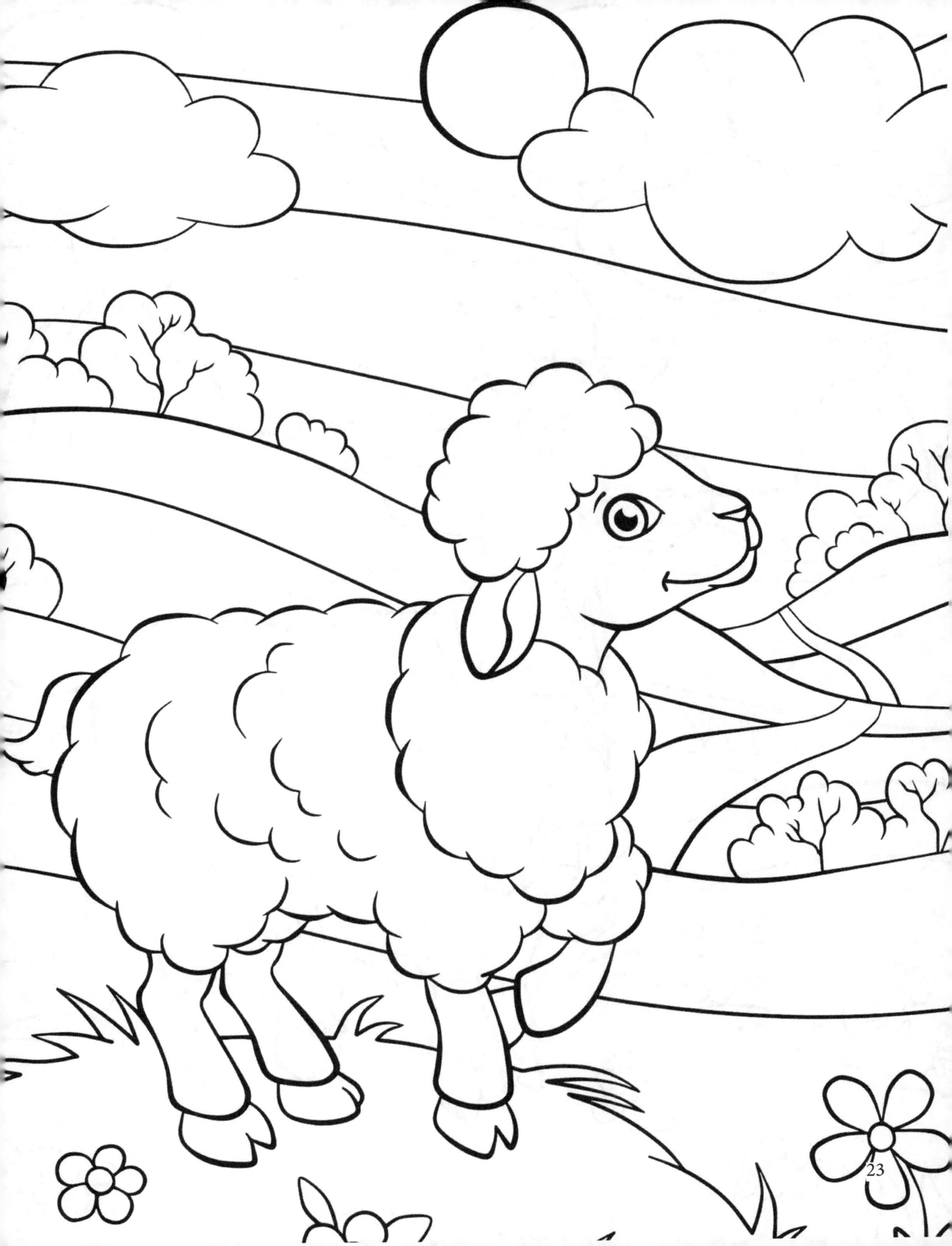

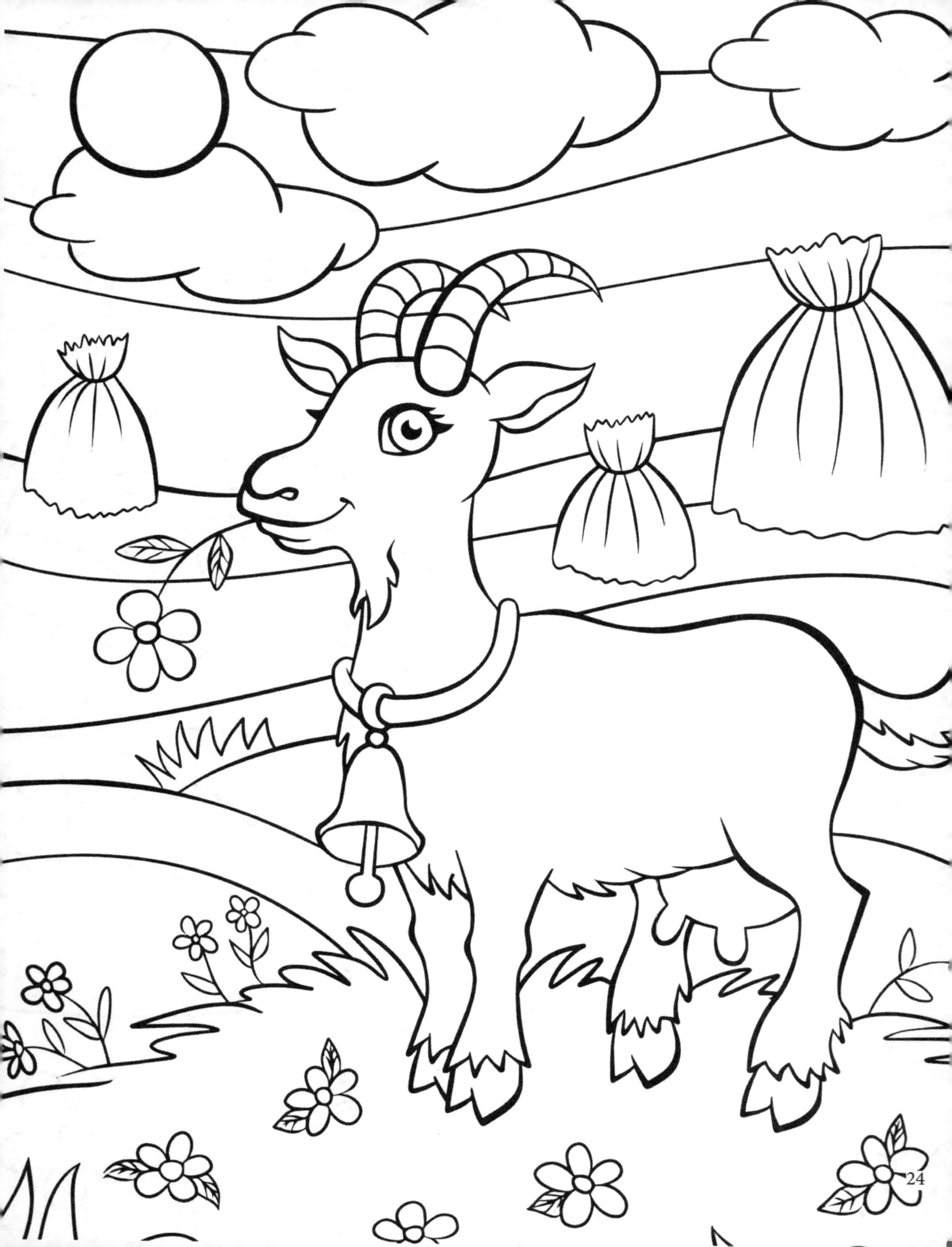

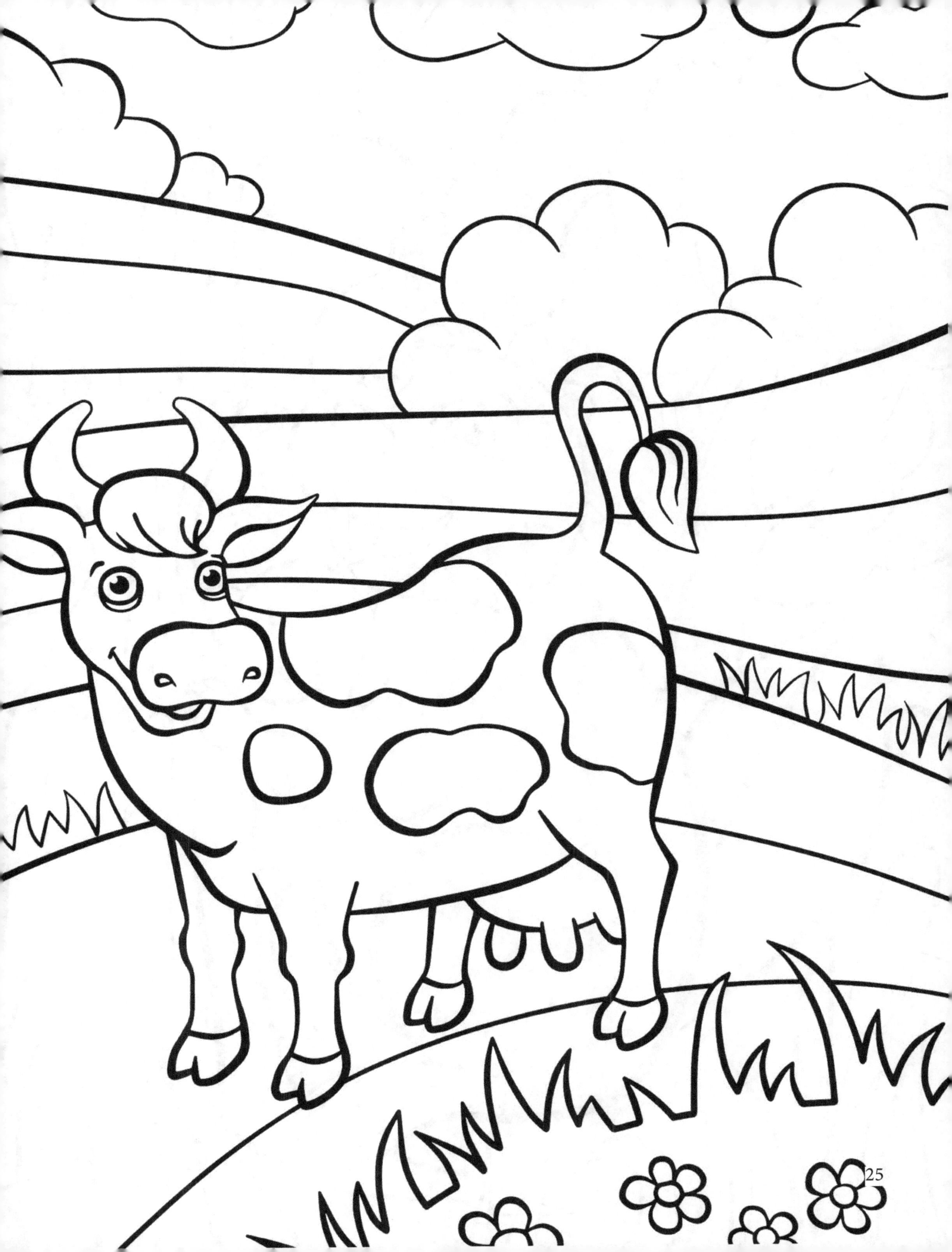

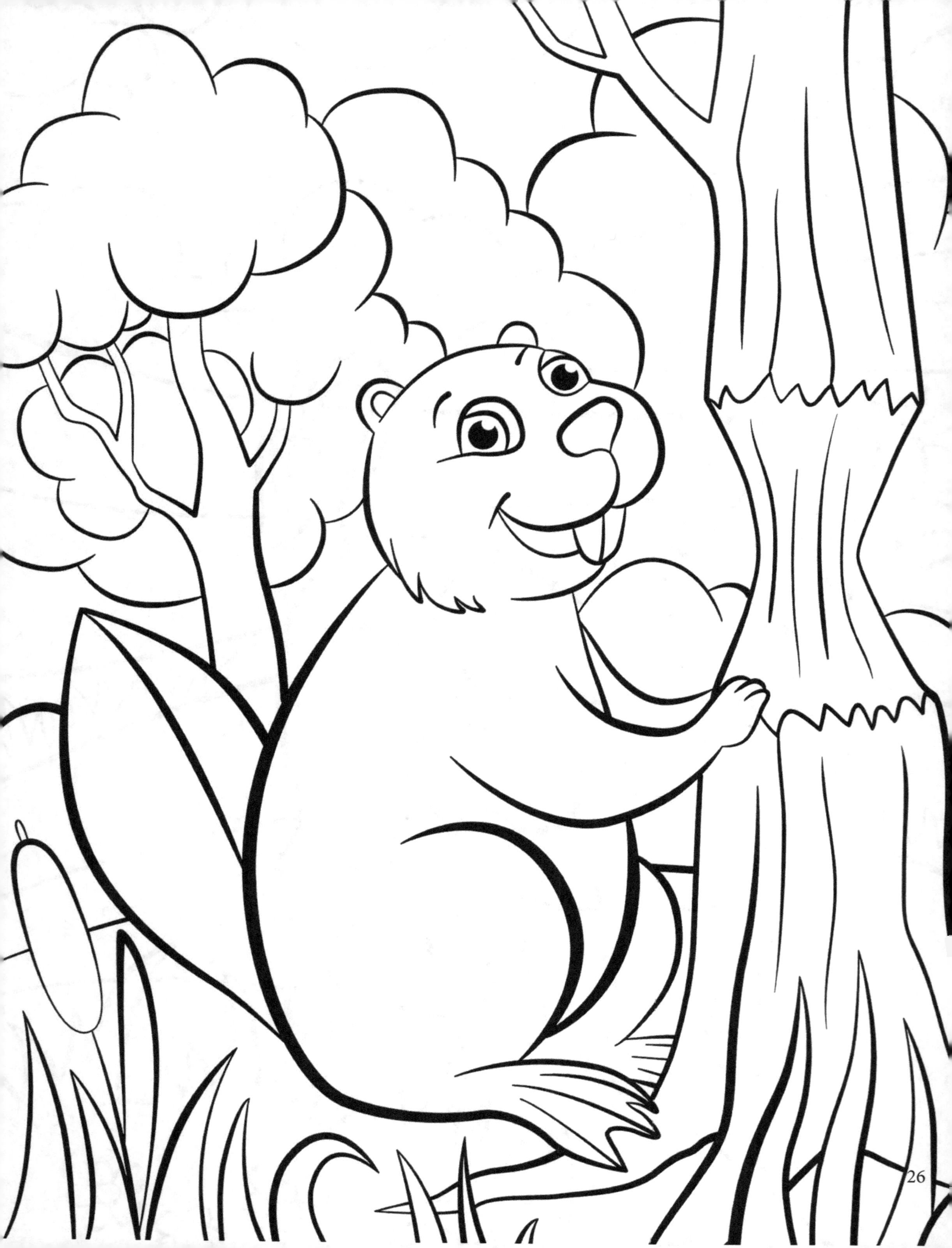

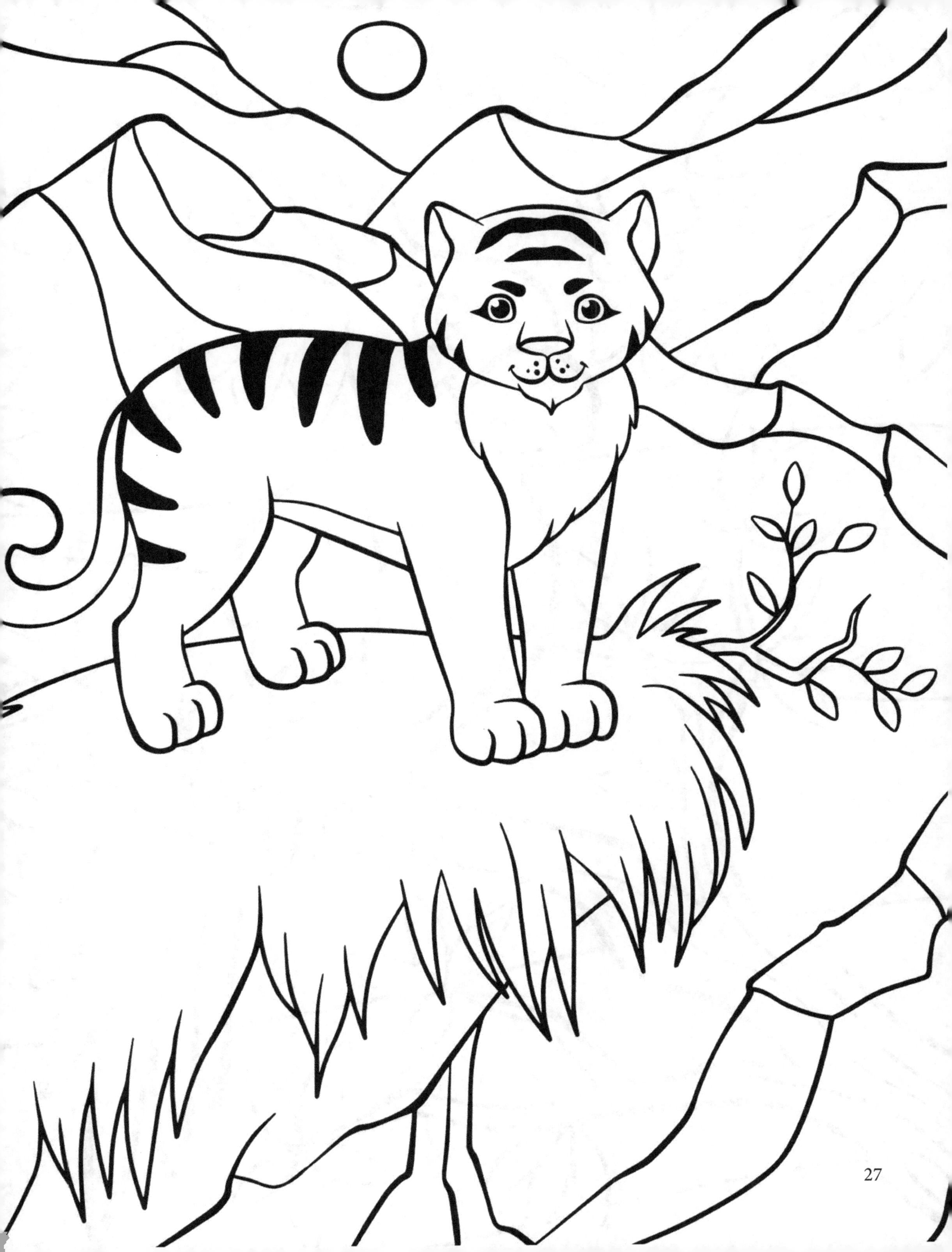

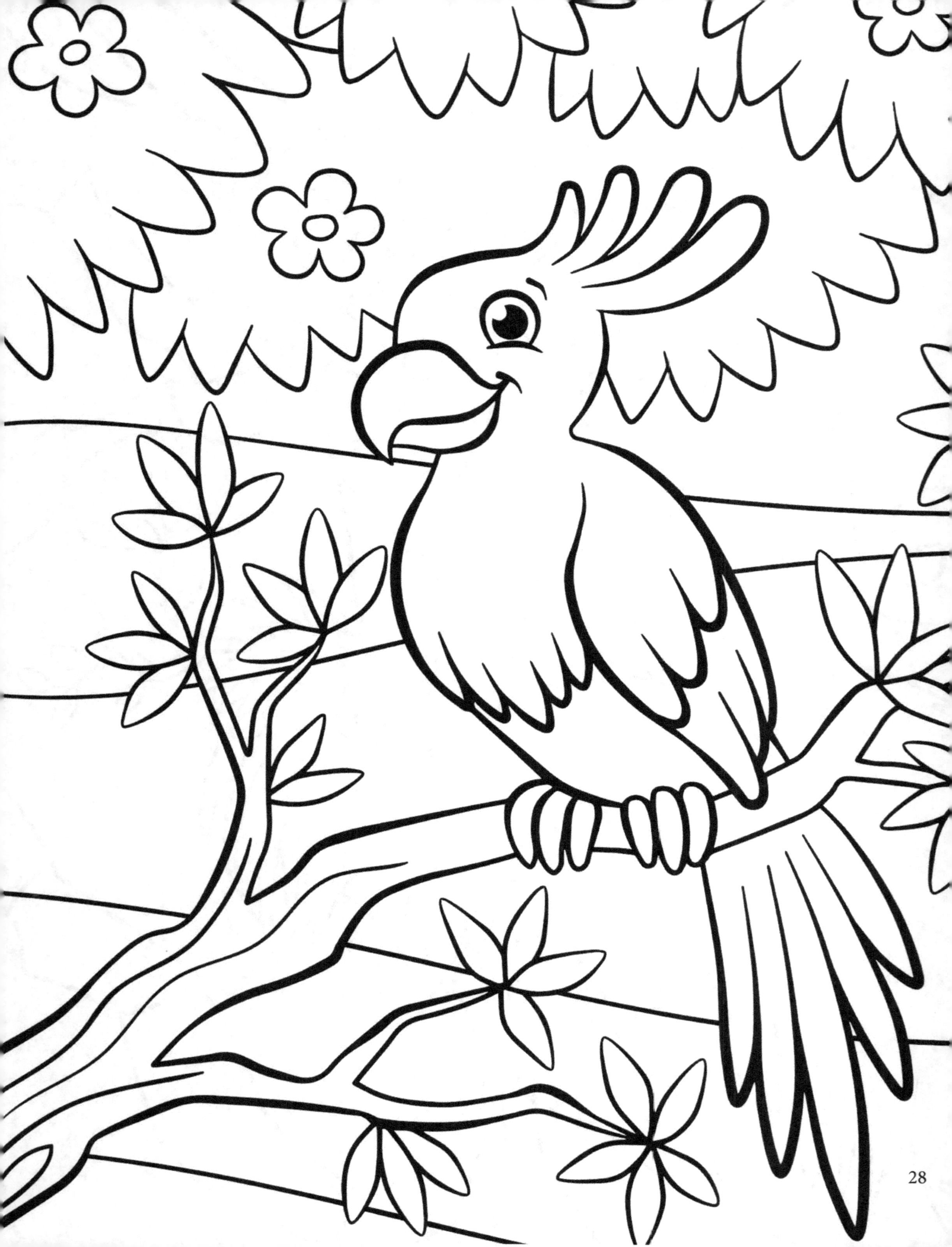

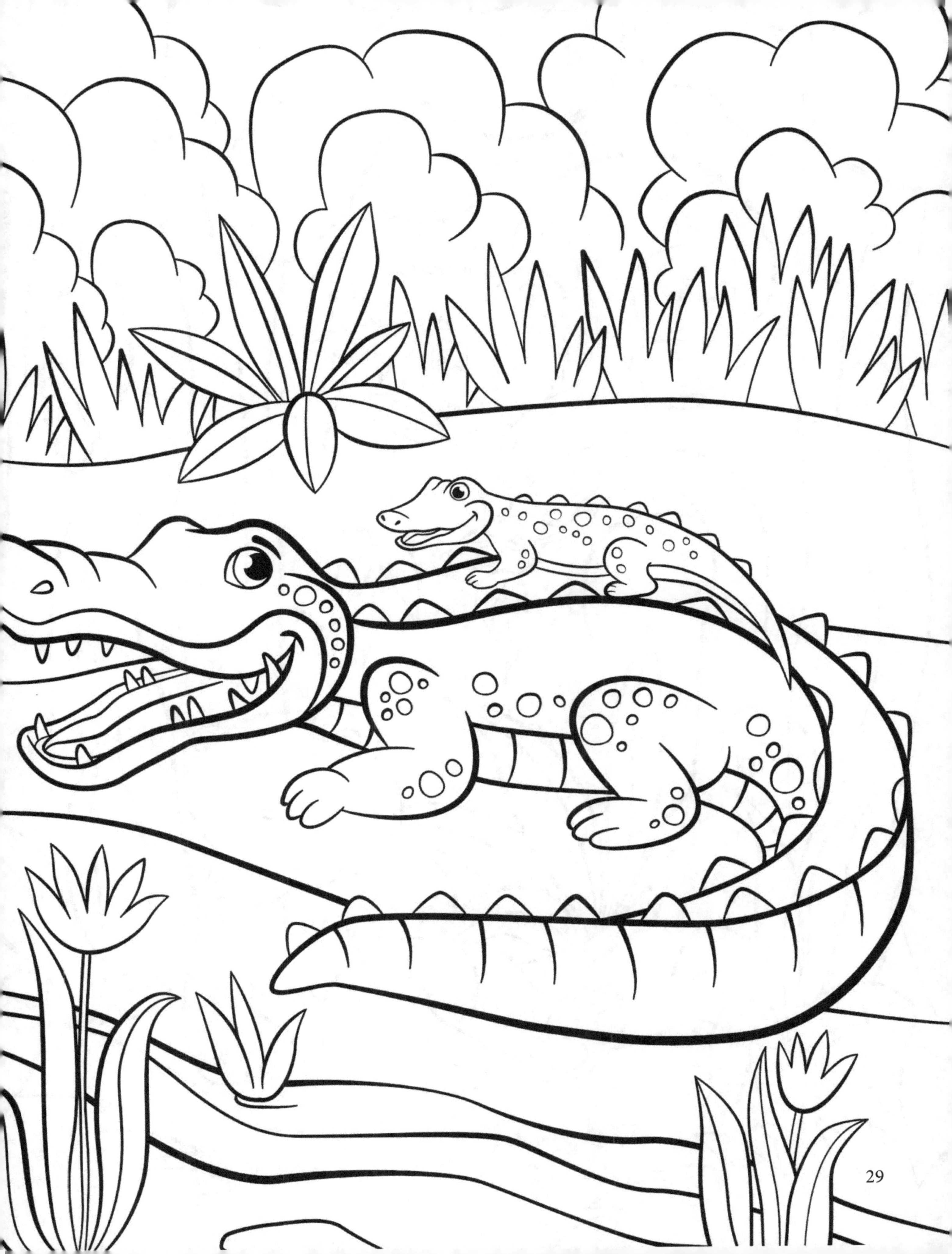

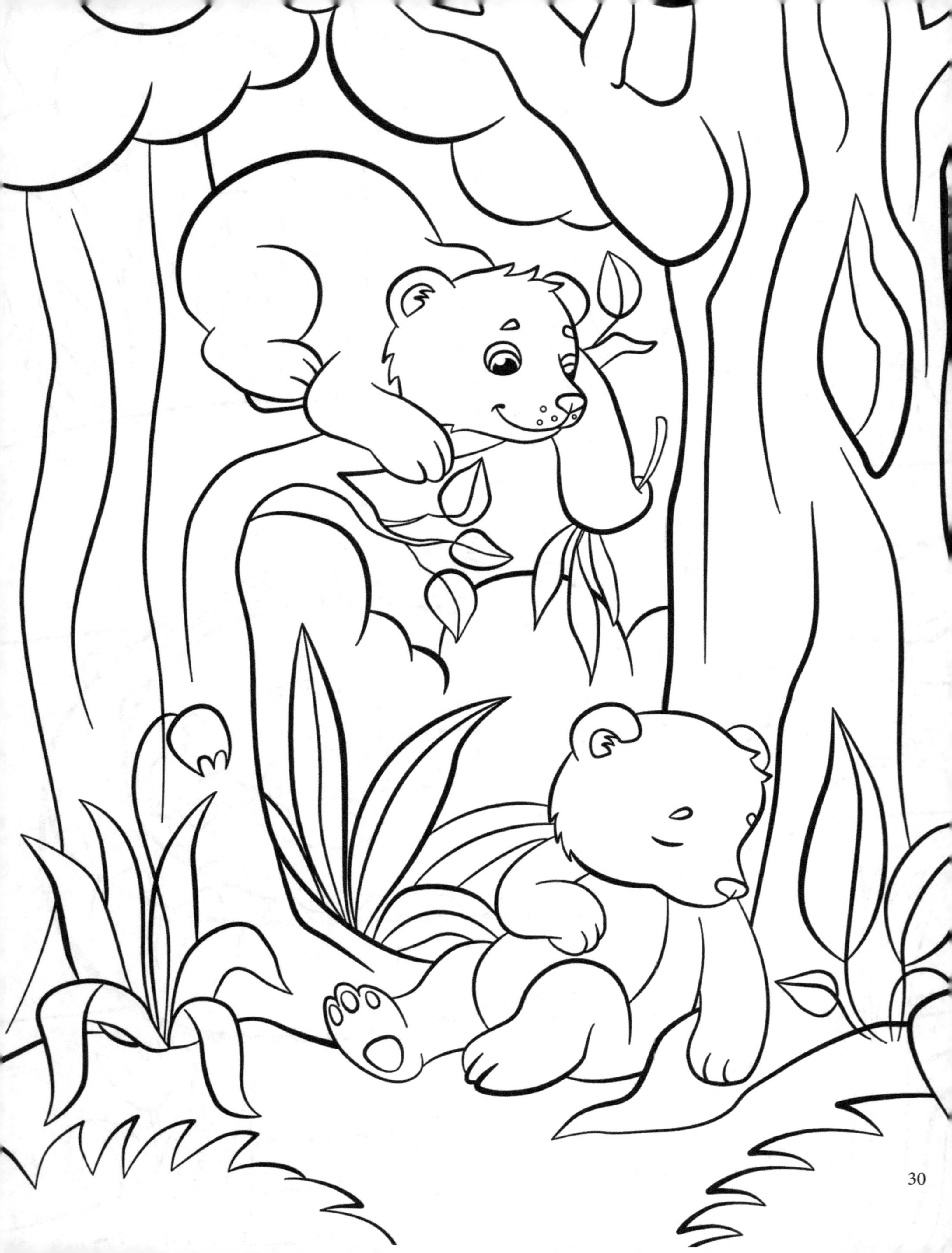

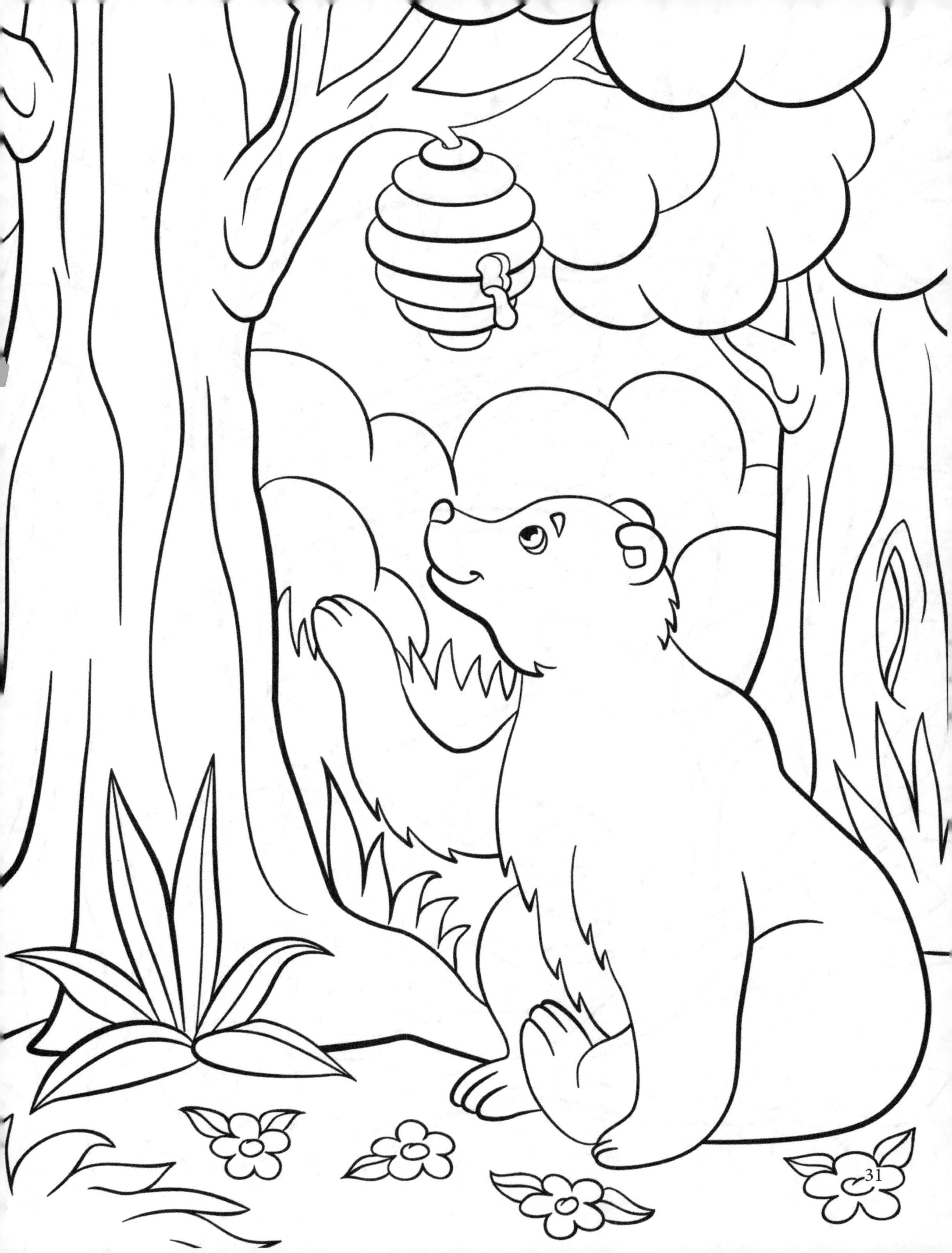

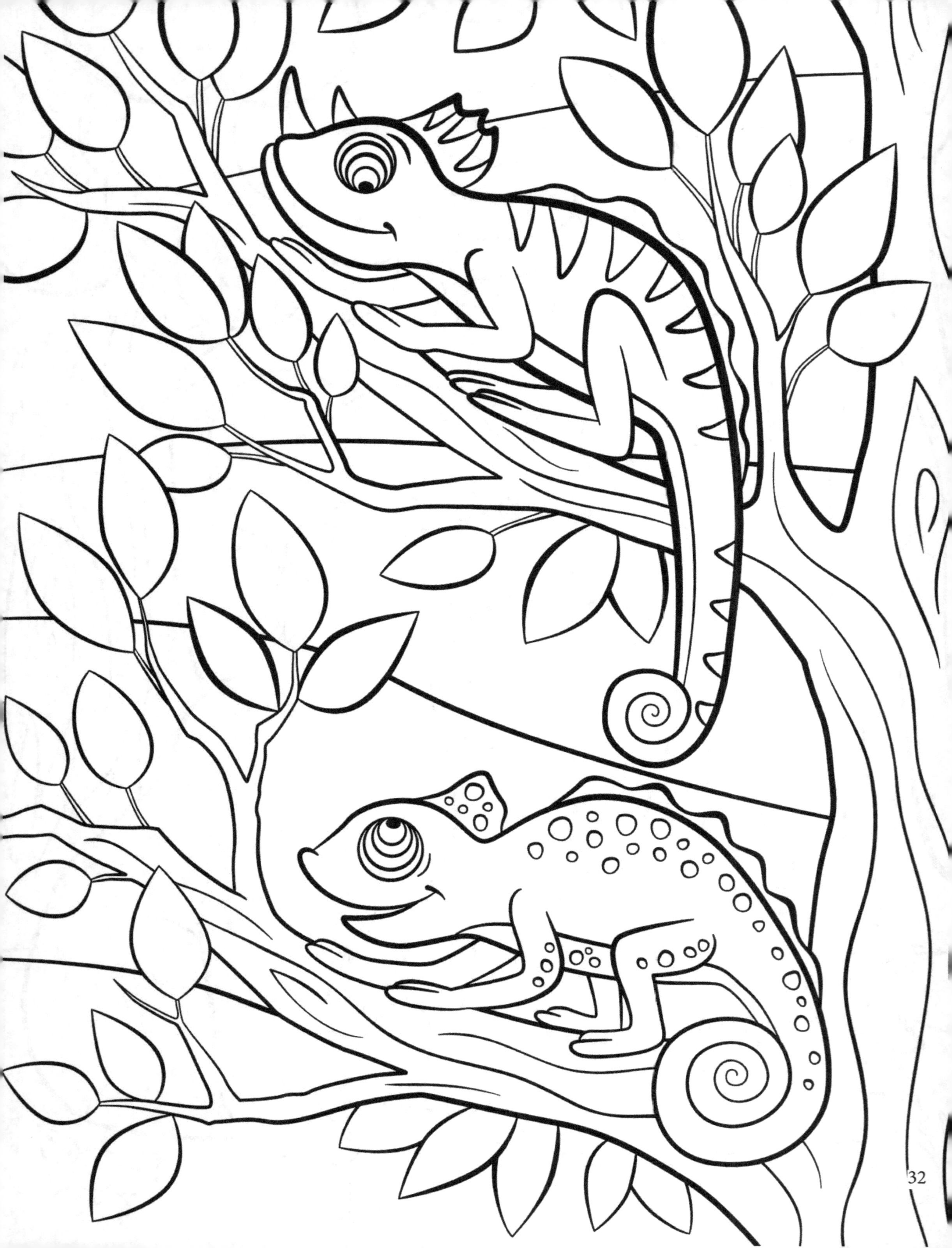

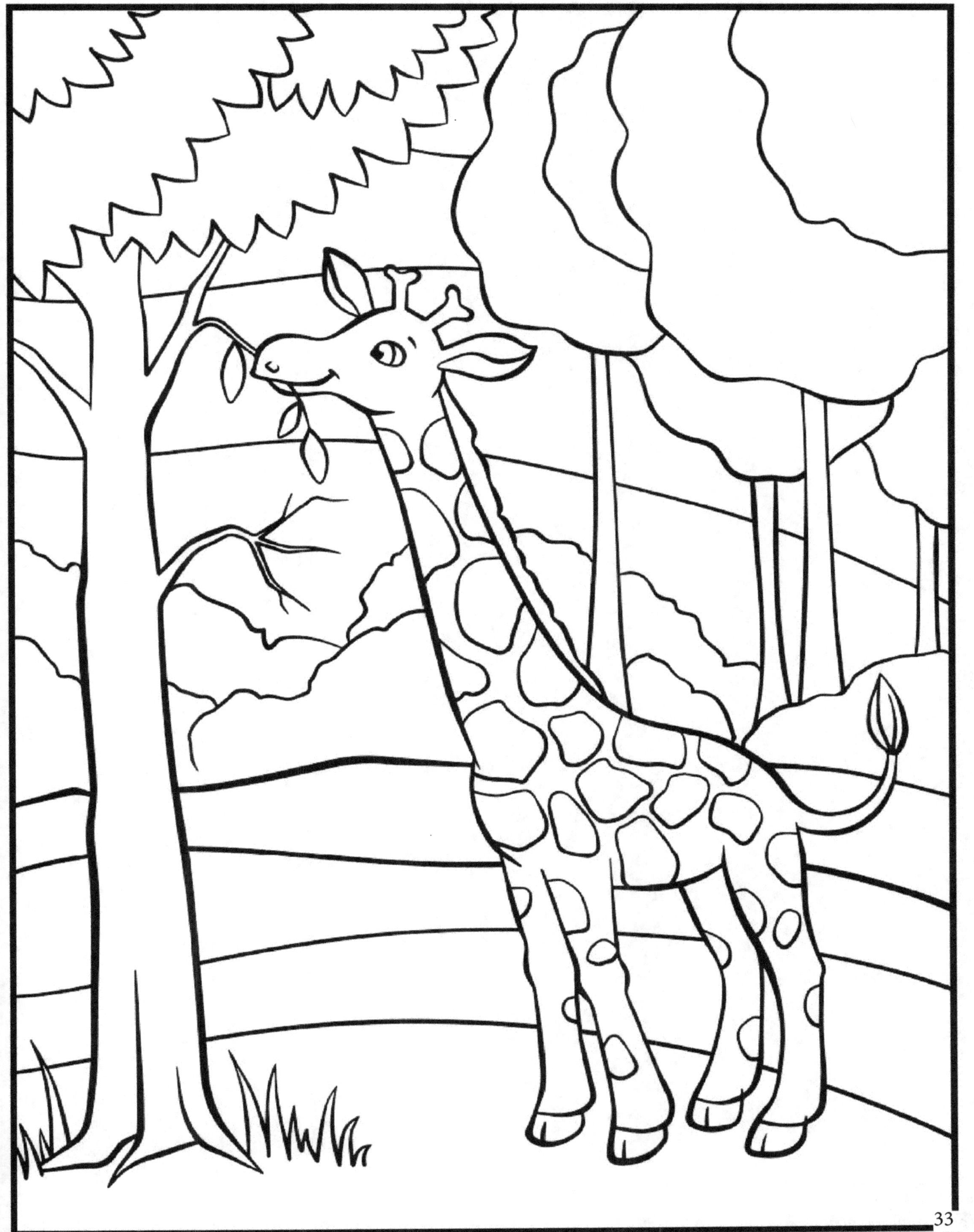